Palgrave Studies in Digital Business & Enabling Technologies

Series Editor
Theo Lynn
Irish Centre for Cloud Computing (IC4)
Dublin City University
Dublin, Ireland

This multi-disciplinary series will provide a comprehensive and coherent account of cloud computing, social media, mobile, big data, and other enabling technologies that are transforming how society operates and how people interact with each other. Each publication in the series will focus on a discrete but critical topic within business and computer science, covering existing research alongside cutting edge ideas. Volumes will be written by field experts on topics such as cloud migration, measuring the business value of the cloud, trust and data protection, fintech, and the Internet of Things. Each book has global reach and is relevant to faculty, researchers and students in digital business and computer science with an interest in the decisions and enabling technologies shaping society.

More information about this series at
http://www.palgrave.com/gp/series/16004

Theo Lynn • John P. Morrison
David Kenny
Editors

Heterogeneity, High Performance Computing, Self-Organization and the Cloud

palgrave
macmillan

Editors
Theo Lynn
Irish Centre for Cloud Computing
(IC4)
Dublin City University
Dublin, Ireland

John P. Morrison
Department of Computer Science
University College Cork
Cork, Ireland

David Kenny
Dublin City University
Dublin, Dublin, Ireland

Palgrave Studies in Digital Business & Enabling Technologies
ISBN 978-3-319-76037-7   ISBN 978-3-319-76038-4   (eBook)
DOI 10.1007/978-3-319-76038-4

Library of Congress Control Number: 2018941797

Cover pattern © Melisa Hasan

Printed on acid-free paper

This Palgrave Macmillan imprint is published by the registered company Springer International Publishing AG part of Springer Nature.
The registered company address is: Gewerbestrasse 11, 6330 Cham, Switzerland

PREFACE

This is the first book in the series, "Advances in Digital Business and Enabling Technologies", which aims to contribute to multi-disciplinary research on digital business and enabling technologies, such as cloud computing, social media, big data analytics, mobile technologies, and the Internet of Things, in Europe. This first volume focuses on research that extends conventional thinking on cloud computing architecture design to greater support High Performance Computing (HPC). Meeting the needs of HPC users provides significant challenges to cloud service providers, both technically and culturally, and this book provides a novel approach and indicates a future direction for cloud computing architecture research that may address a significant portion of these challenges. Given the significant role that HPC plays in scientific advancement and the increasing dominance of cloud computing as a global enterprise computing paradigm, this book has value to university educators and researchers, industry, and policy makers.

The content of the book is based on contributions from researchers on the CloudLightning project, a European Union project funded under Horizon 2020 (www.cloudlightning.eu). CloudLightning commenced in 2015 and brought together eight project partners from five countries across Europe to create a new way to provision heterogeneous cloud resources to deliver services, specified by the user, using a bespoke service description language. The goal of CloudLightning is to address energy inefficiencies, particularly in the use of resources, and consequently to deliver savings to the cloud service provider and the cloud consumer in terms of reduced power consumption and improved service delivery, with hyperscale systems particularly in mind. This book is an output of this joint research.

The chapters in the book are organised around key research contributions from CloudLightning. Chapter 1 provides a context for HPC and the cloud, and discusses how heterogeneous cloud computing might provide a solution for certain classes of HPC users. While heterogeneous resources can help address performance concerns of HPC users, it also introduces complexity into an already complex feature space. As such, Chapter 1 also introduces four key design principles used by CloudLightning to address complexity—emergent behaviour, self-organisation, self-management, and the separation of concerns. Chapter 2 presents CloudLightning, a novel heterogeneous cloud computing architecture. Chapters 3 and 4 outline how approaches to resource management, based on self-organisation, self-management, and separation of concerns, help to manage the complexity of the heterogeneous cloud. HPC users are not the only stakeholders whose needs must be met. While HPC users require performance at orders of magnitude greater than the norm, modern cloud service providers require scalability at so-called hyperscale. Chapter 5 discusses the challenges of evaluating the performance of heterogeneous cloud computing architectures at hyperscale and presents a simulation of the proposed solution. The book concludes with a brief discussion of the disruptive potential of the CloudLightning approach both for high performance computing and for hyperscale cloud computing in general.

Dublin, Ireland   Theo Lynn
Cork, Ireland   John P. Morrison
Dublin, Ireland   David Kenny

ACKNOWLEDGEMENTS

This book was partially funded by the European Union's Horizon 2020 Research and Innovation Programme through the CloudLightning project (http://www.cloudlightning.eu) under Grant Agreement Number 643946, and by the Irish Centre for Cloud Computing and Commerce, an Enterprise Ireland and IDA funded technology centre.

CONTENTS

NOTES ON CONTRIBUTORS

Gabriel González Castañé is a postdoctoral researcher in University College of Cork. He holds a PhD in Computer Science in Energy Modelling and Cloud Computing Simulations from University Carlos III of Madrid in 2015. He has participated in several Spanish National Projects and EU projects, where he has undertaken coordination tasks. His interests are cloud computing, distributed systems, modelling and simulation, and self-management and self-organising cloud computing systems.

Dapeng Dong is a senior postdoctoral researcher with Department of Computer Science at University College Cork, Ireland, where he received his PhD degree in Computer Science and the master degree in Software and Systems for Mobile Networks. He is also a Cisco Certified Network Engineer in Routing and Switching, a Microsoft Certified System Engineer, a Sun Microsystems Certified Java Programmer, Web Component Developer, and Business Component Developer. His research focuses on cloud computing, data compression, and efficient big data analytics and systems.

Ioan Dragan is a teaching assistant at Victor Babes University of Medicine and Pharmacy, Timisoara, Romania. Also, he is a postdoctoral researcher at the e-Austria Research Institute in Timişoara. He received his PhD in Computer Science from Vienna University of Technology, Vienna, Austria, in 2015. His research interests include first-order logic, formal verification, digital image processing and cloud computing, with recent focus on cloud monitoring techniques, orchestration and configuration management.

Christos Filelis-Papadopoulos received his PhD in High-Performance Scientific Computations from the Department of Electrical and Computer Engineering of Democritus University of Thrace in 2014 and is working as a researcher. His research interests include preconditioned iterative methods, multigrid and multilevel methods as well as parallel computing.

Teodor-Florin Fortiş is an associate professor in the Department of Computer Science at West University of Timişoara, Romania. Also, he is a senior researcher at the e-Austria Research Institute in Timişoara, Romania. He received his PhD in Computer Science from West University of Timişoara, Romania, in 2001. His research interests include Formal Languages, Web and Workflow Technologies, Service-Oriented Computing, and Cloud Computing.

Konstantinos M. Giannoutakis is a postdoctoral research fellow at the Information Technologies Institute of Centre for Research and Technology Hellas. His research interests include high performance and scientific computing, parallel systems, grid/cloud computing, service-oriented architectures and software engineering techniques. His articles have appeared in over 60 publications in the above research areas.

George A. Gravvanis is a professor in the Department of Electrical and Computer Engineering of Democritus University of Thrace. His research interests include computational methods, mathematical modelling and applications, and parallel computations. He has published over 200 papers and is a member of the editorial board of international journals.

David Kenny is the project manager of the CloudLightning project, with University College Cork. A certified Professional Scrum Master, Kenny holds a Bachelor of Arts (Hons) degree in International Business and Japanese and a MSc in E-Commerce (Business) from Dublin City University.

Charalampos S. Kouzinopoulos is a postdoctoral research fellow at the Information Technologies Institute of Centre for Research and Technology Hellas. Prior to that he was a senior research fellow at CERN and a researcher at the University of Macedonia. His research interests include parallel and distributed applications across various parallel platforms including clusters and multicore processors using MPI, OpenMP, pthreads, ZeroMQ and NanoMSG, GPGPU computing using the CUDA and OpenCL APIs, high-performance computing, pattern-matching algorithms, Bioinformatics, High Energy Physics and Big Data.

Theo Lynn is Professor of Digital Business at Dublin City University and is the Principal Investigator (PI) of the Irish Centre for Cloud Computing and Commerce, an Enterprise Ireland/IDA-funded Cloud Computing Technology Centre. Professor Lynn specialises in the role of digital technologies in transforming business processes. He is the PI on the Horizon 2020 CloudLightning and RECAP projects.

Antonios T. Makaratzis is a research assistant at the Information Technologies Institute of Centre for Research and Technology Hellas. His research is focused on scientific computing, sparse matrix algorithms, cloud computing and parallel computing.

John P. Morrison is the coordinator of the H2020 CloudLightning project. He is the founder and director of the Centre for Unified Computing. He is a co-founder and director of the Boole Centre for Research in Informatics, a co-founder and co-director of Grid-Ireland and Principal Investigator in the Irish Centre for Cloud Computing and Commerce. Prof. Morrison has held a Science Foundation of Ireland Principal Investigator award and has published widely in the field of Parallel Distributed and Grid Computing. He has been the guest editor on many journals including the *Journal of SuperComputing*, *Future Generation Computing Systems* and the *Journal of Scientific Computing*. He has served on dozens of international conference programme committees and is a co-founder of the International Symposium on Parallel and Distributed Computing.

Marian Neagul is a lecturer in the Department of Computer Science at West University of Timişoara, Romania. Also, he is a postdoctoral researcher at the e-Austria Research Institute in Timişoara, Romania. He received his PhD in Computer Science from West University of Timişoara, Romania, in 2015. His research interests include distributed systems, computer networks and operating systems, with recent focus on Cloud Computing, particularly orchestration, deployment and configuration management.

Dana Petcu is Professor of Distributed and Parallel Computing in the Department of Computer Science at West University of Timisoara and a senior researcher at the e-Austria Research Institute in Timisoara. Her latest scientific contributions are referring to Cloud, Grid or Cluster computing. She has also undertaken several management tasks and acts as the editor-in-chief of *Scalable Computing: Practice and Experience*.

Teodora Selea is a PhD student at West University of Timisoara, Romania. She is a junior researcher at the e-Austria Research Institute in Timisoara, Romania. Her research interests include distributed computing and artificial intelligence.

Adrian Spătaru is a PhD student at West University of Timisoara and a junior researcher at the e-Austria Research Institute in Timisoara. Adrian's research topics include distributed systems, artificial intelligence and their integration. During the past four years he gained experience in Cloud Computing, related to orchestration, deployment and provisioning. Recent research directions focus on timeseries prediction and Cloud-Blockchain integration. Adrian participated in research projects starting with FP7 SCAPE (related to scalable digital preservation environments), FP7 SPECS (Security as a Service in cloud computing) and H2020 CloudLightning. Adrian was awarded an IBM BSRE Certificate in 2014, also being present four years in a row (2012–2015) at ACM ICPC SEERC (South-Eastern-European leg at the collegiate programming contest) in Bucharest.

Dimitrios Tzovaras is a senior researcher and director at the Information Technologies Institute of Centre for Research and Technology Hellas. His main research interests include visual analytics, data fusion, biometric security, virtual reality, machine learning and artificial intelligence. He has authored over 110 articles in refereed journals and over 290 papers in international conferences.

Huanhuan Xiong is a senior postdoctoral researcher in University College Cork. She received a BSc in Economics from Wuhan University of Technology (Wuhan, China) in 2004, an MSc in Software Engineering and a PhD in Geographic Information System (GIS) from Wuhan University (Wuhan, China) in 2006 and 2012. She worked in IC4 (Irish Centre for Cloud Computing & Commerce) for three years, and she has expertise in cloud migration, cloud architecture, cloud interoperability and scalability. Her research interests include cloud architecture, game theory, self-organised and self-optimised systems.

LIST OF ABBREVIATIONS

3D	Three dimensional
AMD	Advanced Micro Devices
API	Application Programming Interface
ARM	Advanced Reduced Instruction Set Computing Machine
AWS	Amazon Web Services
BDaaS	Big Data as as Service
BIOS	Basic Input/Output System
CAMP	Cloud Application Management for Platforms
CL	CloudLightning
CL-SDL	CloudLightning Service Description Language
CM	Cell Manager
CPU	Central Processing Unit
CRM	Customer Relationship Management
CSAR	Cloud Service Archive
CSP	Cloud Service Provider
DDR	Double Data Rate
DES	Discrete Event Simulators
DFE	Data Flow Engine
DNA	Deoxyribonucleic Acid
DSP	Digital Signal Processor
DUNE	Distributed and Unified Numeric Environment
EAD	Enterprise Application Developer
EAO	Enterprise Application Operator
ERP	Enterprise Resource Planning
FLOPs	Floating Point Operations per Second
FPGA	Field-Programmable Gate Array
GDP	Gross Domestic Product

GPGPU	General Purpose GPU
GPU	Graphical Processing Unit
GUI	Graphical User Interface
HA	High Availability
HAL	Hardware Abstraction Layer
HOT	Heat Orchestration Template
HPC	High Performance Computing
HPCaaS	High Performance Computing as a Service
HTC	High Throughput Computing
I/O	Input/Output
IaaS	Infrastructure as a Service
IBM	International Business Machines
ICT	Information and Communications Technologies
IDC	International Data Corporation
IP	Internet Protocol
IT	Information Technology
MAPE-K	Monitor-Analyse-Plan-Execute-Knowledge
MIC	Many Integrated Core
MIPS	Million instructions per second
MP	Message Passing
MPI	Message Passing Interface
MQ	Message Queue
NAS	Network Attached Storages
NIC	Network Interface Cards
NIST	National Institute of Standards and Technology
NUMA	Non-uniform Memory Access
OASIS	Organization for the Advancement of Structured Information Standards
OPM	Open Porous Media
PaaS	Platform as a Service
PLS	Packet-Level Simulators
PnP	Plug and Play/Plug & Play
pRouter	Prescription Router
pSwitch	Prescription Switch
QoS	Quality of Service
R&D	Research and Development
RAL	Resource Abstraction Layer
RAM	Random Access Memory
RTM	Real-Time Migration
SaaS	Software as a Service
SDE	Service Decomposition Engine
SDL	Service Description Language

SI	Suitability Index
SLA	Service-Level Agreement
SOSM	Self-Organisation Self-Management
SPEC	Standard Performance Evaluation Corporation
SSL	Secure Sockets Layer
ToR	Top-of-Rack
TOSCA	Topology and Orchestration Specification for Cloud Applications
UI	User Interface
VM	Virtual Machine
VPN	Virtual Private Networks
vRM	Virtual Rack Manager
WSC	Warehouse Scale Computer
YAML	Yet Another Markup Language

LIST OF FIGURES

LIST OF TABLES

Addressing the Complexity of HPC in the Cloud: Emergence, Self-Organisation, Self-Management, and the Separation of Concerns

Theo Lynn

Abstract New use scenarios, workloads, and increased heterogeneity combined with rapid growth in adoption are increasing the management complexity of cloud computing at all levels. High performance computing (HPC) is a particular segment of the IT market that provides significant technical challenges for cloud service providers and exemplifies many of the challenges facing cloud service providers as they conceptualise the next generation of cloud architectures. This chapter introduces cloud computing, HPC, and the challenges of supporting HPC in the cloud. It discusses how heterogeneous computing and the concepts of self-organisation, self-management, and separation of concerns can be used to inform novel cloud architecture designs and support HPC in the cloud at hyperscale.

T. Lynn (✉)
Irish Centre for Cloud Computing (IC4), Dublin City University,
Dublin, Ireland
e-mail: theo.lynn@dcu.ie

© The Author(s) 2018
T. Lynn et al. (eds.), *Heterogeneity, High Performance Computing, Self-Organization and the Cloud*, Palgrave Studies in Digital Business & Enabling Technologies,
https://doi.org/10.1007/978-3-319-76038-4_1

Three illustrative application scenarios for HPC in the cloud—(i) oil and gas exploration, (ii) ray tracing, and (iii) genomics—are discussed.

Keywords Cloud computing • High performance computing • Emergent systems • Self-organising systems • Self-managing systems • Heterogeneous computing

1.1   INTRODUCTION

The objective of this book is to introduce readers to CloudLightning, an architectural innovation in cloud computing based on the concepts of self-organisation, self-management, and separation of concerns, showing how it can be used to support high performance computing (HPC) in the cloud at hyperscale. The remainder of this chapter provides a brief overview of cloud computing and HPC, and the challenges of using the cloud for HPC workloads. This book introduces some of the major design concepts informing the CloudLightning architectural design and discusses three challenging HPC applications—(i) oil and gas exploration, (ii) ray tracing, and (iii) genomics.

1.2   CLOUD COMPUTING

Since the 1960s, computer scientists have envisioned global networks delivering computing services as a utility (Garfinkel 1999; Licklider 1963). The translation of these overarching concepts materialised in the form of the Internet, its precursor ARPANET, and more recently cloud computing. The National Institute of Standards and Technology (NIST) defines cloud computing as:

> ...*a model for enabling ubiquitous, convenient, on-demand network access to a shared pool of configurable computing resources (e.g., networks, servers, storage, applications, and services) that can be rapidly provisioned and released with minimal management effort or service provider interaction.*
> (Mell and Grance 2011, p. 2)

NIST defines cloud computing as having five essential characteristics, three service models, and four deployment models as per Table 1.1.

Since the turn of the decade, the number and complexity of cloud providers offering one or more of the primary cloud service models—

Table 1.1 Cloud computing essential characteristics, service models, and deployment models (adapted from Mell and Grance 2011)

	Essential characteristics
On-demand self-service	Consumers can unilaterally provision computing capabilities as needed automatically without requiring human interaction with the cloud provider.
Broad network access	Capabilities are available over the network and accessed through standard mechanisms that promote use by heterogeneous thin or thick client platforms and interfaces (e.g. devices).
Resource pooling	The provider's computing resources are pooled to serve multiple consumers using a multi-tenant model, with different physical and virtual resources dynamically assigned and reassigned according to consumer demand.
Rapid elasticity	Capabilities can be elastically provisioned and released, in some cases automatically, to scale rapidly outwards and inwards to meet demand. To the consumer, the capabilities available for provisioning often appear to be unlimited and can be appropriated in any quantity at any time.
Measured service	Cloud systems automatically control and optimise resource use by leveraging a metering capability at some level of abstraction appropriate to the type of service. Resource usage can be monitored, controlled, and reported, providing transparency to the service provider and the consumer.
	Service models
Software as a Service	The capability provided to a consumer to use a provider's applications running on a cloud infrastructure and accessible by client interface.
Platform as a Service	The capability provided to a consumer to deploy onto the cloud infrastructure consumer-created or acquired applications created using development technologies provided by the provider.
Infrastructure as a Service	The capability provided to a consumer to provision computing resources to deploy and run arbitrary software such as operating systems and applications.
	Deployment models
Private Cloud	The cloud infrastructure is provisioned for exclusive use by a single organisation comprising multiple consumers. Ownership, management, and operation of the infrastructure may be done by one or more of the organisations in the community, by a third party, or a combination of both, and it may exist on or off premise.
Community Cloud	The cloud infrastructure is provisioned for exclusive use by a specific community of consumers from organisations that have shared concerns. Ownership, management, and operation of the infrastructure may be done by one or more of the organisations in the community, by a third party, or a combination of both, and it may exist on or off premise.

(continued)

Table 1.1 (continued)

Public Cloud	The cloud infrastructure is provisioned for open use by the general public. It may be owned, managed, and operated by a business, academic, or government organisation, or some combination of them. It exists on the premises of the cloud provider.
Hybrid Cloud	The cloud infrastructure is a composition of two or more distinct cloud infrastructures (private, community, or public) that remain unique entities, but are bound together by standardised or proprietary technology that enables data and application portability.

Infrastructure-as-a-Service (IaaS), Platform-as-a-Service (PaaS), and Software-as-a-Service—as private, public, community, and hybrid clouds has increased. Cloud computing is now considered to be the dominant computing paradigm in enterprise Information Technology (IT) and the backbone of many software services used by the general public, including search, email, social media, messaging, and storage. Enterprises are attracted by the convergence of two major trends in IT—IT efficiencies and business agility, enabled by scalability, rapid deployment, and parallelisation (Kim 2009). Figure 1.1 summarises the strategic motivations for cloud adoption.

Despite its ubiquity, cloud computing is dominated by a small number of so-called hyperscale cloud providers, companies whose underlying cloud infrastructure and revenues from cloud services are at a different order of magnitude to all the others. These include companies who offer a wide range of cloud services such as Microsoft, Google, Amazon Web Services (AWS), IBM, Huawei and Salesforce.com, as well as companies whose core businesses leverage the power of cloud to manage the scale of their, typically online, operations such as Facebook, Baidu, Alibaba and eBay. Estimates suggest that such companies operate one to three million or more servers worldwide (Data Center Knowledge 2017; Clark 2014). Research by Cisco (2016) suggests that these hyperscale operators number as little as 24 companies operating approximately 259 data centres in 2016. By 2020, these companies will account for 47% of all installed data centre servers and 83% of the public cloud server installed base (86% of public cloud workloads) serving billions of users worldwide (Cisco 2016).

The data centres operated by hyperscale cloud service providers are sometimes referred to as Warehouse Scale Computers (WSCs) to differentiate them from other data centres. The data centre(s) hosting WSCs are typically not shared. They are operated by one organisation to run a small number

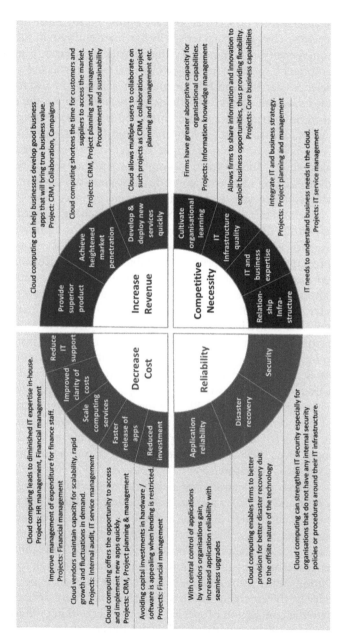

Fig. 1.1 IC4 cloud computing strategic alignment model

of high-use applications or services, and are optimised for those applications and services. They are characterised by hardware and system software platform homogeneity, a common systems management layer, a greater degree of proprietary software use, single organisation control, and a focus on cost efficiency (Barroso and Hölzle 2007). It is important also to note that for these hyperscale clouds, the clouds, per se, sit on top of the physical data centre infrastructure and are abstracted from end-user applications, end users, and software developers exploiting the cloud. Indeed, hyperscale clouds operate across multiple data centres typically organised by geographic region. This abstraction, combined with homogeneity, provides cloud service providers with cost efficiencies and deployment flexibility allowing cloud service providers to maintain, enhance, and expand the underlying cloud infrastructure without requiring changes to software (Crago and Walters 2015). Conventionally, cloud computing infrastructure performance is improved through a combination of scale-out and natural improvements in microprocessor capability, while service availability is assured through over-provisioning. As a result, hyperscale data centres are high-density facilities utilising tens of thousands of servers and often measure hundreds of thousands of square feet in size. For example, the Microsoft data centre in Des Moines, Iowa, is planned to occupy over 1.2 million square feet in size when it opens in 2019. While this high-density homogeneous scale-out strategy is effective, it results in significant energy costs. Servers may be underutilised relative to their peak load capability, with frequent idle times resulting in disproportionate energy consumption (Barroso and Hölzle 2007; Awada et al. 2014). Furthermore, the scale of data centre operations results in substantial cooling-related costs, with significant cost and energy impacts (Awada et al. 2014). Unsurprisingly, given their focus on cost effectiveness, power optimisation is a priority for WSC operators.

From a research perspective, WSCs introduce an additional layer of complexity over and above smaller-scale computing platforms due to the larger scale of the application domain (including an associated deeper and less homogeneous storage hierarchy), higher fault rates, and possibly higher performance variability (Barroso and Hölzle 2007). This complexity is further exacerbated by the dilution of homogeneity through technological evolution and an associated evolving set of use cases and workloads. More specifically, the emergence of new specialised hardware devices that can accelerate the completion of specific tasks and networking infrastructure that can support higher throughput and lower latency is enabling support for workloads that traditionally would be considered HPC (Yeo and Lee 2011). The introduction of heterogeneity combined with new workloads, such as those classified as HPC, will further introduce greater system performance variability, including response times and, as a result, will impact the quality of service. As such, new approaches to provisioning are required. Despite these challenges, cloud service providers have sought to enter the HPC market catering largely for batch processing workloads that are perfectly or pleasingly parallelisable. Examples include AWS Batch, Microsoft Azure Batch, and Google Zync Render. Notwithstanding the entry of these major cloud players, cloud is one of the smallest segments in the HPC market and vice versa (Intersect360 Research 2014)

1.3   HIGH PERFORMANCE COMPUTING

HPC typically refers to computer systems that through a combination of processing capability and storage capacity rapidly solve difficult computational problems (Ezell and Atkinson 2016). Here, performance is governed by the (effective) processing speed of the individual processors and the time spent in inter-processor communications (Ray et al. 2004). As technology has evolved, processors have become faster, can be accelerated, and can be exploited by new techniques. Today, HPC systems use parallel processing achieved by deploying grids or clusters of servers and processors in a scale-out manner or by designing specialised systems with high numbers of cores, large amounts of total memory, and high-throughput network connectivity (Amazon Web Services 2015). The top tier of these specialised HPC systems are supercomputers whose cost can reach up to US$100 million. Such supercomputers are measured in floating-point operations per second (FLOPS) rather than millions of instructions per second, the measurement of processing capacity in general-purpose computing. At the time of writing, the world's fastest supercomputer, the Chinese Sunway TaihuLight, has over 10 million cores and a LINPACK benchmark rating of 93 petaflops (Feldman 2016; Trader 2017) and a peak performance of 125 petaflops (National Supercomputing Centre, WuXi n.d.). It is estimated to have cost US$273 million (Dongarra 2016).

Traditionally, HPC systems are typically of two types—Message passing (MP)-based systems and Non-uniform Memory Access (NUMA)-based systems. MP-based systems are connected using scalable, high-bandwidth, low-latency inter-node communications (interconnect) (Severance and

Dowd 2010). Instead of using the interconnect to pass messages, NUMA systems are large parallel processing systems that use the interconnect to implement a distributed shared memory that can be accessed from any processor using a load/store paradigm (Severance and Dowd 2010). In addition to HPC systems, HPC applications can be organised into three categories—tightly coupled, loosely coupled, and data intensive. The stereotypical HPC applications run on supercomputers are typically tightly coupled and written using the messaging passing interface (MPI) or shared memory programming models to support high levels of inter-node communication and high performance storage (Amazon Web Services 2015). Weather and climate simulations or modelling for oil and gas exploration are good examples of tightly coupled applications. Loosely coupled applications are designed to be fault tolerant and parallelisable across multiple nodes without significant dependencies on inter-node communication or high performance storage (Amazon Web Services 2015). Three-dimensional (3D) image rendering and Monte Carlo simulations for financial risk analysis are examples of loosely coupled applications. A third category of HPC application is data-intensive applications. These applications may seem similar to the loosely coupled category but are dependent on fast reliable access to large volumes of well-structured data (Amazon Web Services 2015). More complex 3D-animation rendering, genomics, and seismic processing are exemplar applications.

HPC plays an important role in society as it is a cornerstone of scientific and technical computing including biological sciences, weather and climate modelling, computer-aided engineering, and geosciences. By reducing the time to complete the calculations to solve a complex problem and by enabling the simulation of complex phenomenon, rather than relying on physical models or testbeds, HPC both reduces costs and accelerates innovation. Demand and interest in HPC remain high because problems of increasing complexity continue to be identified. Society values solving these problems, and the economics of simulation and modelling is believed to surpass other methods (Intersect360 Research 2014). As such, it is recognised as playing a pivotal role in both science discovery and national competitiveness (Ezell and Atkinson 2016). International Data Corporation (IDC), in a report commissioned for the European Commission, highlights the importance of HPC:

> *The use of high performance computing (HPC) has contributed significantly and increasingly to scientific progress, industrial competitiveness, national and*

regional security, and the quality of human life. HPC-enabled simulation is widely recognized as the third branch of the scientific method, complementing traditional theory and experimentation. HPC is important for national and regional economies—and for global ICT collaborations in which Europe participates—because HPC, also called supercomputing, has been linked to accelerating innovation.

(IDC 2015, p. 20)

Despite the benefits of HPC, widespread use of HPC has been hampered by the significant upfront investment and indirect operational expenditure associated with running and maintaining HPC infrastructures. The larger supercomputer installations require an investment of up to US$1 billion to operate and maintain. As discussed, performance is the overriding concern for HPC users. HPC machines consume a substantial amount of energy directly and indirectly to cool the processors. Unsurprisingly, heat density and energy efficiency remain a major issue and has a direct dependence on processor type. Increasingly, the HPC community is focusing beyond mere performance to performance per watt. This is particularly evident in the Green500 ranking of supercomputers.[1] Cursory analysis of the most energy efficient supercomputers suggests that the use of new technologies such as Graphical Processing Units (GPUs) results in significant energy efficiencies (Feldman 2016). Other barriers to greater HPC use include recruitment and retention of suitably qualified HPC staff. HPC applications often require configuration and optimisation to run on specialised infrastructure; thus, staff are required not only to maintain the infrastructure but to optimise software for a specific domain area or use case.

1.4   HPC and the Cloud

At first glance, one might be forgiven for thinking that HPC and cloud infrastructures are of a similar hue. Their infrastructure, particularly at Warehouse Scale, is distinct from the general enterprise, and both parallelisation and scalability are important architectural considerations. There are high degrees of homogeneity and tight control. However, the primary emphasis is very different in each case. The overriding focus in HPC is performance and typically optimising systems for a small number of large workloads. Tightly coupled applications, such as those in scientific computing, require parallelism and fast connections between processors to meet performance requirements (Eijkhout et al. 2016). Performance is improved through vertical scaling. Where workloads are data intensive, data locality also becomes an issue, and therefore, HPC systems often require any given server in its system to be not only available and operative but connected via high-speed, high-throughput, and low-latency network interconnects. The advantages of virtualisation, and particularly space and time multiplexing, are of no particular interest to the HPC user (Mergen et al. 2006). Similarly, cost effectiveness is a much lower consideration.

In contrast, the primary focus in cloud computing is scalability and not performance. In general, systems are optimised to cater for multiple tenants and a large number of small workloads. In cloud computing, servers also must be available and operational, but due to virtualisation, the precise physical server that executes a request is not important, nor is the speed of the connections between processors provided the resource database remains coherent (Eijkhout et al. 2016). As mentioned earlier, unlike HPC, the cloud is designed to scale quickly for perfectly or pleasingly parallel problems. Cloud service providers, such as AWS, are increasingly referring to these types of workloads as High Throughput Computing (HTC) to distinguish them from traditional HPC on supercomputers. Tasks within these workloads can be parallelised easily, and as such, multiple machines and applications (or copies of applications) can be used to support a single task. Scalability is achieved through horizontal scaling—the ability to increase the number of machines or virtual machine instances. Cost effectiveness is a key consideration in cloud computing.

So, while there are technical similarities between the hyperscale cloud service providers operating their own Warehouse Scale Computing systems and HPC end users operating their own supercomputer systems, the commercial reality is the needs of HPC end users are not aligned with the traditional operating model of cloud service providers, particularly for tightly coupled use cases. Why? HPC end users, driven by performance, want access to heterogeneous resources including different accelerators, machine architectures, and network interconnects that may be unavailable from cloud service providers, obscured through virtualisation technologies, and/or impeded by multi-locality (Crago et al. 2011). The general cloud business model assumes minimal capacity for the end user to interfere in the physical infrastructure underlying its cloud and to exploit space and time multiplexing through virtualisation to achieve utilisation and efficiency gains. The challenge for service providers and HPC end users is one of balancing the need for (i) performance and scalability and

(ii) maximum performance and minimal interference. CloudLightning argues that this can be achieved through architectural innovation and the exploitation of heterogeneity, self-organisation, self-management, and separation of concerns.

1.5 Heterogeneous Computing

As discussed earlier, cloud computing data centres traditionally leverage homogeneous hardware and software platforms to support cost-effective high-density scale-out strategies. The advantages of this approach include uniformity in system development, programming practices, and overall system capability, resulting in cost benefits to the cloud service provider. In the case of cloud computing, homogeneity typically refers to a single type of commodity processor. However, there is a significant cost to this strategy in terms of energy efficiency. While transistors continued to shrink, it has not been possible to lower the processor core voltage levels to similar degrees. As a result, cloud service providers have significant energy costs associated not only with over-provisioning but with cooling systems. As such, limitations on power density, heat removal, and related considerations require a different architecture strategy for improved processor performance than adding identical, general-purpose cores (Esmaeilzadeh et al. 2011; Crago and Walters 2015).

Heterogeneous computing refers to architectures that allow the use of processors or cores, of different types, to work efficiently and cooperatively together using shared memory (Shan 2006; Rogers and Fellow 2013). Unlike traditional cloud infrastructure built on the same processor architecture, heterogeneity assumes use of different or dissimilar processors or cores that incorporate specialised processing capabilities to handle specific tasks (Scogland et al. 2014; Shan 2006). Such processors, due to their specialised capabilities, may be more energy efficient for specific tasks than general-purpose processors and/or can be put in a state where less power is used (or indeed deactivated if possible) when not required, thus, maximising both performance and energy efficiency (Scogland et al. 2014). GPUs, many integrated cores (MICs), and data flow engines (DFEs) are examples of co-processor architectures with relatively positive computation/power consumption ratios.[2] These architectures support heterogeneous computing because they are typically not standalone devices but are rather considered as co-processors to a host processor. As mentioned previously, the host processor can complete one instruction stream, while the co-processor can complete a different instruction stream or type of stream (Eijkhout et al. 2016).

Modern GPUs are highly parallel programmable processors with high computation power. As can be derived from their name, GPUs were originally designed to help render images faster; however, wider adoption was hindered by the need for specialised programming knowledge. GPUs have a stream processing architecture fundamentally different than the widely known Intel general-purpose Central Processing Unit (CPU) programming models, tools, and techniques. As general-purpose GPU programming environments matured, GPUs were used for a wider set of specialist processing tasks including HPC workloads (Owens et al. 2007; Shi et al. 2012). Intel's Many-Integrated Core (MIC) architecture seeks to combine the compute density and energy efficiency of GPUs for parallel workloads without the need for a specialised programming architecture; MICs make use of the same programming models, tools, and techniques as those for Intel's general-purpose CPUs (Elgar 2010). DFEs are fundamentally different to GPUs and MICs in that they are designed to efficiently process large volumes of data (Pell and Mencer 2011). A DFE system typically contains, but is not restricted to, a field-programmable gate array (FPGA) as the computation fabric and provides the logic to connect an FPGA to the host, Random Access Memory for bulk storage, interfaces to other buses and interconnects, and circuitry to service the device (Pell et al. 2013). FPGAs are optimised processors for non-floating-point operations and provide better performance and energy efficiency for processing large volumes of integer, character, binary, and fixed point data (Proaño et al. 2014). Indeed, DFEs may be very inefficient for processing single values (Pell and Mencer 2011). A commonly cited use case for DFEs is high-performance data analytics for financial services. In addition to their performance, GPUs, MICs, and DFEs/FPGAs are attractive to HPC end users as they are programmable and therefore can be reconfigured for different use cases and applications. For example, as mentioned earlier, GPUs are now prevalent in many of the world's most powerful supercomputers.

It should be noted that while heterogeneity may provide higher computation/power consumption ratios, there are some significant implementation and optimisation challenges given the variance in operation and performance characteristics between co-processors (Teodoro et al. 2014). Similarly, application operation will depend on data access and the processing patterns of the co-processors, which may also vary by application and co-processor type (Teodoro et al. 2014). For multi-tenant cloud computing, these challenges add to an already complex feature space where processors may not easily support virtualisation or where customers may require bare-metal provisioning thereby restricting resource pooling (Crago et al. 2011). For data-intensive application, data transmission to the cloud remains a significant barrier to adoption. Notwithstanding these challenges, cloud service providers have entered the HPC space with specialised processor offerings. For example, AWS now offers CPUs, GPUs, and DFEs/FPGAs, and has announced support for Intel Xeon Phi processors (Chow 2017).

1.6   ADDRESSING COMPLEXITY IN THE CLOUD THROUGH SELF-* DESIGN PRINCIPLES

This chapter previously discussed two computing paradigms—cloud computing and HPC—being driven by end-user demand for greater scale and performance. To achieve these requirements, heterogeneous resources, typically in the form of novel processor architectures, are being integrated into both cloud platforms and HPC systems. A side effect, however, is greater complexity—particularly in the case of hyperscale cloud services where the scale of infrastructure, applications, and number of end users is several orders of magnitude higher than general-purpose computing and HPC. This complexity in such large-scale systems results in significant management, reliability, maintenance, and security challenges (Marinescu 2017). Emergence and the related concept of self-organisation, self-management, and the separation of concerns are design principles that have been proposed as potential solutions for managing complexity in large-scale distributed information systems (Heylighen and Gershenson 2003; Schmeck 2005; Herrmann et al. 2005; Branke et al. 2006; Serugendo et al. 2011; Papazoglou 2012; Marinescu 2017).

The complexity of hyperscale cloud systems is such that it is effectively infeasible for cloud service providers to foresee and manage manually (let alone cost effectively) all possible configurations, component interactions, and end-user operations on a detailed level due to high levels of dynamism in the system. Self-organisation has its roots in the natural sciences and the study of natural systems where it has been long recognised that higher-level outputs in dynamic systems can be an emergent effect of lower-level inputs (Lewes 1875). This is echoed in the field of Computer Science and through Alan Turing's observation that "global order arises from local interactions" (Turing 1952). De Wolf and Holvoet (2004) define emergence as follows:

> *A system exhibits emergence when there are coherent emergent at the macro-level that dynamically arise from the interactions between the parts at the micro-level. Such emergent are novel with regards to the individual parts of the system.*
> (De Wolf and Holvoet 2004, p. 3)

Based on their review of the literature, De Wolf and Holvoet (2004) identify eight characteristics of emergent systems:

1. *Micro-macro effect*—the properties, behaviour, structure, and patterns situated at a higher macro-level that arise from the (inter)actions at the lower micro-level of the systems (so-called emergents).
2. *Radical novelty*—the global (macro-level) behaviour is novel with regard to the individual behaviours at the micro-level.
3. *Coherence*—there must be a logical and consistent correlation of parts to enable emergence to maintain some sense of identity over time.
4. *Interacting parts*—parts within an emergent system must interact as novel behaviour arises from interaction.
5. *Dynamical*—emergents arise as the system evolves over time; new attractors within the system appear over time and as a result new behaviours manifest.
6. *Decentralised control*—no central control directs the macro-level behaviour; local mechanism influences global behaviour.
7. *Two-way link*—there is a bidirectional link between the upper (macro-) and lower (micro-) levels. The micro-level parts interact and give rise to the emergent structure. Similarly, macro-level properties have causal effects on the micro-level.
8. *Robustness and flexibility*—no single entity can have a representation of the global emergent combined with decentralised control implies that no single entity can be a single point of failure. This introduces greater robustness, flexibility, and resilience. Failure is likely to be gradual rather than sudden in emergent systems.

Self-organising systems are similar in nature to emergent systems. Ashby (1947) defined a system as being self-organising where it is "at the same time (a) strictly determinate in its actions, and (b) yet demonstrates a self-induced change of organisation." Heylighen and Gershenson (2003) define organisations as "structure with function" and self-organisation as a functional structure that appears and maintains spontaneously. Again, based on an extensive review of the literature, De Wolf and Holvoet (2004) offer a more precise definition of self-organisation as "a dynamical and adaptive process where systems acquire and maintain structure themselves, without external control." This definition is consistent with Heylighen and Gershenson (2003) while at the same time giving greater insight. De Wolf and Holvoet (2004) synthesise the essential characteristics of self-organising systems as:

1. *Increase in order*—an increase in order (or statistical complexity), through organisation, is required from some form of semi-organised or random initial conditions to promote a specific function.
2. *Autonomy*—this implies the absence of external control or interference from outside the boundaries of the system.
3. *Adaptability or robustness with respect to changes*—a self-organising system must be capable of maintaining its organisation autonomously in the presence of changes in its environment. It may generate different tasks but maintain the behavioural characteristics of its constituent parts.
4. *Dynamical*—self-organisation is a process from dynamism towards order.

The concept of self-organisation is often conflated with emergence, particularly in Computer Science due to the dynamism and robustness inherent in the systems and, frankly, historical similarity of language. While both emergent systems and self-organising systems are dynamic over time, they differ in how robustness is achieved. They can exist in isolation or in combination with each other. For example, Heylighen (1989) and Mamei and Zambonelli (2003) see emergent systems arising as a result of a self-organising process thus implying self-organisation occurs at the micro-level. In contrast, Parunak and Brueckner (2004) consider self-organisation as an effect at the macro-level of emergence as a result of increased order. Sudeikat et al. (2009) note that the systematic design of self-organising systems is scarcely supported and therefore presents a number of challenges to developers including:

- Architectural design including providing self-organising dynamics as software components and application integration
- Methodological challenges including conceptual but practical means for designing self-organising dynamics by refining coordination strategies and supporting validation of explicit models for self-organised applications

Despite these challenges, De Wolf and Holvoet (2004) conclude for hugely complex systems "...we need to keep the individuals rather simple and let the complex behaviour self-organise as an emergent behaviour from the interactions between these simple entities."

The concept of self-management is much more well defined in the Computer Science literature and has its roots in autonomic computing (Zhang et al. 2010). The concept of autonomic computing was popularised by IBM in a series of articles starting in 2001 with Horn's "Autonomic Computing: IBM's Perspective on the State of Information Technology." These ideas were further elaborated by Kephart and Chess (2003) and Ganek and Corbi (2003) amongst others. For IBM, autonomic computing was conceptualised as "computing systems that can manage themselves given high-level objectives from administrators" (Kephart and Chess 2003). Kephart and Chess (2003) further elaborated the essence of autonomic computing systems through four aspects of self-management—self-configuration, self-optimisation, self-healing, and self-protection. In line with autonomic computing, the function of any self-management is the use of control or feedback loops, such as Monitor-Analyse-Plan-Execute-Knowledge (MAPE-K), that collect details from the system and act accordingly, anticipating system requirements and resolving problems with minimal human intervention (Table 1.2) (IBM 2005).

The so-called self-* aspects of IBM's vision of autonomic computing are used in a wide range of related advanced technology initiatives and have been extended to include self-awareness, self-monitoring, and self-adjustment (Dobson et al. 2010). Despite the significant volume of research on self-management, like self-organisation, implementation of self-management presents significant challenges. These include issues related to the application of the agent-oriented paradigm, designing a component-based approach (including composition formalisms) for supporting self-management, managing relationships between autonomic elements, distribution and decentralisation at the change management layer, design and implementation of robust learning and optimisation techniques, and robustness in a changing environment (Kramer and Magee 2007; Nami et al. 2006).

Research on the application of the principles of emergence, self-organisation, and self-management is widely referenced in Computer Science literature, typically discretely. There are few significant studies on architectures combining such principles. One such example is that of the Organic Computing project funded by the German Research Foundation (DFG). This research programme focused on understanding emergent global behaviour in "controlled" self-organising systems with an emphasis on distributed embedded systems (Müller-Schloer et al. 2011). However, for cloud computing architectures, there are relatively few examples. This is not to say that there is a dearth of applications of these concepts for specific cloud computing functions. There are numerous examples of bio-inspired algorithms for task scheduling (e.g. Li et al. 2011; Pandey et al. 2010), load balancing (Nishant et al. 2012), and other cloud-related functions. Similarly, Guttierez and Sim (2010) describe a self-organising agent system for service composition in the cloud. However, these are all at the sub-system level. The relatively few cloud architectural studies, other than those relating to CloudLightning, are all the more surprising given that some commentators, notably, Zhang et al. (2010), posit that cloud computing systems are inherently self-organising. Such a proposition is not to

Table 1.2 Self-management aspects of autonomic computing (adapted from Kephart and Chess 2003)

Concept	Description	Benefit
Self-configuration	Automated configuration of components and systems follows high-level policies. Rest of system adjusts automatically and seamlessly.	Increased responsiveness
Self-optimization	Components and systems continually seek opportunities to improve their own performance and efficiency.	Increased operational efficiencies
Self-healing	System automatically detects, diagnoses, and repairs localised software and hardware problems.	Increased resilience
Self-protection	System automatically defends against malicious attacks or cascading failures. It uses early warning to anticipate and prevent system-wide failures.	Increased security

dismiss self-management in cloud computing outright. Indeed, Zhang et al. (2010) admit that cloud computing systems exhibit autonomic features. However, a more purist interpretation suggests that these are not self-managing and do not explicitly aim to reduce complexity. Marinescu et al. (2013) emphasises the suitability of self-organisation as a design principle for cloud computing systems proposing an auction-driven self-organising cloud delivery model based on the tenets of autonomy of individual components, self-awareness, and intelligent behaviour of individual components including heterogeneous resources. Similarly, while self-management has been applied at a sub-system or node level (e.g. Brandic 2009), there are few studies on large-scale self-managing cloud architectures. One such system-level study is Puviani and Frei (2013) who, building on Brandic (2009), propose a catalogue of adaptation patterns based on requirements, context, and expected behaviour. These patterns are classified according to the service components and autonomic managers. Control loops following the MAPE-K approach enact adaptation. In their approach, each service component is autonomous and autonomic and has its own autonomic manager that monitors itself and the environment. The service is aware of changes in the environment including new and disappearing components and adapts on a negotiated basis with other components to meet system objectives. While Puviani and Frei (2013) and Marinescu et al. (2013) propose promising approaches, they are largely theoretical and their conclusions lack the data from real implementations.

While emergence, self-organisation, and self-management may prove to be principles for reducing overall system complexity, for a HPC use case, the issue of minimal interference remains. At the same time, surveys of the HPC end-user community emphasise the need for "ease of everything" in the management of HPC (IDC 2014). To create a service-oriented architecture that can cater for heterogeneous resources while at the same time shielding deployment and optimisation effort from the end user is not insignificant. As discussed, it is counter-intuitive to the conventional general-purpose model, which, in effect, is one-size-fits-all for end users. Separation of concerns is a concept that implements a "what-how" approach cloud architectures separating application lifecycle management and resource management. The end user, HPC, or otherwise, focuses its effort on what needs to be done, while the cloud service provider concentrates on how it should be done. In this way, the technical details for interacting with cloud infrastructure are abstracted away and instead the end user or enterprise application developer provides (or selects) a detailed deployment plan including constraints and quality of service parameters using a service description language and service delivery model provided by the cloud service provider, a process known as blueprinting. Blueprinting empowers an "end-user-centric view" by enabling end users to use highly configurable service specification templates as building blocks to (re) assemble cloud applications quickly while at the same time maintain minimal interference with the underlying infrastructure (Papazoglou 2012). While there are a number of existing application lifecycle frameworks for PaaS (e.g. Apache Brooklyn and OpenStack Solum) and resource frameworks for IaaS (OpenStack Heat) that support blueprints, neither the blueprints nor the service delivery models have been designed to accommodate emergence, self-organisation, or self-management.

1.7   APPLICATION SCENARIOS

It is useful when reading further, to have one or more use cases in mind that might benefit from HPC in the cloud and more specifically a novel cloud computing architecture to exploit heterogeneity and self-* principles. Three motivating use cases are presented: (i) oil and case exploration, (ii) ray tracing, and (iii) genomics. These fall into the three HPC application categories discussed earlier, that is, tightly coupled applications, loosely coupled applications, and data-intensive applications. In each case, an architecture exploiting heterogeneous resources and built on the principles of self-organisation, self-management, and separation of concerns is anticipated to offer greater energy efficiency. By exploiting heterogeneous computing technologies, the performance/cost and performance/watt are anticipated to improve significantly. In addition, heterogeneous resources will enable computation to be hosted at hyperscale in the cloud, making large-scale compute-intensive applications and by-products accessible and practical from a cost and time perspective for a wider group of stakeholders. In each use case, even relatively small efficiency and accuracy gains can result in competitive advantage for industry.

1.7.1   *Oil and Gas Exploration*

The oil and gas industry makes extensive use of HPC to generate images of earth's subsurface from data collected from seismic surveys as well as compute-intensive reservoir modelling and simulations. Seismic surveys are performed by sending sound pulses into the earth or ocean, and recording the reflection. This process is referred to as a "shot". To generate images in the presence of complex geologies, a computationally intensive process called Real-Time Migration (RTM) can be used. RTM operates on shots, and for each shot, it runs a computationally and data-expensive wave propagation calculation and a cross-correlation of the resulting data to generate an image. The images from each shot are summed to create an overall image. Similarly, the Open Porous Media (OPM) framework is used for simulating the flow and transport of fluids in porous media and makes use of numerical methods such as Finite Elements, Finite Volumes, Finite Differences, amongst others. These processes and simulations typically have not been operated in the cloud because of (a) data security, (b) data movement, and (c) poor performance. At the same time, on-site in-house HPC resources are often inadequate due to the "bursty" nature of processes where peak demand often exceeds compute resources. RTM and OPM are exemplars of tightly coupled applications.

One solution to address challenges and objections related to poor performance is to use a self-organising, self-managing cloud infrastructure to harness larger compute resources efficiently to deliver more energy and cost-efficient simulations of complex physics using OPM/Distributed and Unified Numeric Environment (DUNE). As well as supporting greater cloud adoption for HPC in the oil and gas sector, the development of a convenient scalable cloud solution in this space can reduce the risk and costs of dry exploratory wells. Relatively small efficiency and accuracy gains in simulations in the oil and gas industry can result in disproportionately large benefits in terms of European employment and Gross Domestic Product (GDP).

1.7.2   Ray Tracing

Ray tracing is widely used in image processing applications, such as those used in digital animation productions where the development of an image from a 3D scene is achieved by tracing the trajectories of light rays through pixels in a view plane. In recent years, the advancement of HPC and new algorithms has enabled the processing of large numbers of computational tasks in a much smaller time. Consequently, ray tracing has become a potential application for interactive visualisations. Ray tracing is commonly referred to as an "embarrassingly parallelisable algorithm" and is naturally implemented in multicore shared memory systems and distributed systems. It is an example of a loosely coupled application.

Ray tracing has applications in a wide variety of industries including:

• Image rendering for high resolution and 3D images for the animation and gaming industry
• Human blockage modelling in radio wave propagation studies and for general indoor radio signal prediction
• Atmospheric radio wave propagation
• Modelling solar concentrator designs to investigate performance and efficiency
• Modelling laser ablation profiles in the treatment of high myopic astigmatism to assess the efficacy, safety, and predictability
• Development of improved ultrasonic array imaging techniques in anisotropic materials
• Ultrasonic imaging commonly used in inspection regimes, for example, weld inspections
• Modelling Light-emitting diode (LED) illumination systems

These industries have significant scale, and they increasingly rely on computationally intensive image processing, accelerated by innovations in consumer electronics, for example, HDTV and 3D TV. A variety of ray tracing libraries exist that are optimised for MIC and GPU platforms, for example, Intel Embree and NVIDIA Optix.

1.7.3   Genomics

Genomics is the study of all of a person's genes (the genome), including interactions of those genes with each other and with the person's environment. Since the late 1990s, academic and industry analysts have identified the potential of genomics to realise significant gains in development time and reduced investment, largely attached to realising efficiency gains. Genomics provides pharmaceutical companies with long-term upside and competitive advantage through savings right along the Research and Development (R&D) value chain (including more efficient target discovery, lead discovery, and development) but also in better decision-making accuracy resulting from more, better, and earlier information which ultimately results in higher drug success rates (Boston Consulting Group 2001). The net impact is that genomics can result in more successful drug discovery. Relatively small efficiency and accuracy gains in the pharmaceutical industry can result in disproportionately large benefits in terms of employment and GDP. However, genome processing requires substantial computational power and storage requiring significant infrastructure and specialist IT expertise. While larger organisations can afford such infrastructure, it is a significant cost burden for smaller pharmaceutical companies, hospitals and health centres, and researchers. Even when such an infrastructure is in place, researchers may be stymied by inadequate offsite access.

Genomics has two core activities:

- *Sequencing*: a laboratory-based process involving "reading" deoxyribonucleic acid (DNA) from the cells of an organism and digitising the results
- *Computation*: the processing, sequence alignment, compression, and analysis of the digitised sequence

Historically, the cost of sequencing has represented the most significant percentage of the total. However, this cost has decreased dramatically over the past decade due to breakthroughs in research and innovation in that area. As the cost of sequencing has dropped, the cost of computation (alignment, compression, and analysis) has formed a greater proportion of the total. The biggest consumer of compute runtime is sequence alignment—assembling the large number of individual short "reads" which come out of the sequencer (typically, a few hundred bases long) into a single complete genome. This can be split into many processing jobs, each processing batches of reads and aligning against a reference genome, and run in parallel. Significant input data is required, but there is little or no inter-node communication needed. The most computationally intensive kernel in the overall process is local sequence alignment, using algorithms such as Smith Waterman, which is very well suited to being optimised through the use of heterogeneous compute technologies such as DFEs.

Genome processing is an exemplar of a data-intensive application. Greater energy efficiency is anticipated from using heterogeneous computing resulting in lower costs. As the cost of the raw sequencing technology drops, the computing challenge becomes the final significant technology bottleneck preventing the routine use of genomics data in clinical settings. Not only can the use of heterogeneous computing technologies offer significantly improved performance/cost and performance/

watt, but enabling this computation to be hosted at large-scale in the cloud makes it practical for wide-scale use. In addition to realigning the computation cost factors in genome processing with sequencing costs, a HPC solution can significantly improve the genome processing through-put and speed of genome sequence computation thereby reducing the wider cycle time thus increasing the volume and quality of related research. The benefits of such a cloud solution for genome processing are obvious. Researchers, whether in large pharmaceutical companies, genomics research centres, or health centres, can invest their energy and time in R&D and not managing and deploying complex on-site infrastructure.

1.8   Conclusion

This chapter introduces two computing paradigms—cloud computing and HPC, both of which are being impacted by technological advances in het-erogeneous computing but also hampered by energy inefficiencies and increasing complexity. A combination of self-organisation, self-management, and the separation of concerns is proposed as design principles for a new hyperscale cloud architecture that can exploit the opportunities presented by heterogeneity to deliver more energy-efficient cloud computing and, in particular, support HPC in the cloud.

This book presents CloudLightning, a new way to provision heteroge-neous cloud resources to deliver services, specified by the user, using a bespoke service description language. As noted, self-organising and self-managing systems present significant architecture design, methodological, and development challenges. These challenges are exacerbated when com-bined and considered at hyperscale. The remainder of this book presents CloudLightning's response to these challenges illustrating the utilisation of concepts in emergence, self-organisation, self-management, and the separation of concerns in a reference architecture for hyperscale cloud computing (Chap. 2).

Chapter 3 describes the self-organising and self-management formal-isms designed to support coordination mechanisms within the CloudLightning architecture. As discussed earlier, stakeholders in cloud computing, and specifically HPC end users, have different concerns, for example, enterprise application developers and end users may want greater control over application lifecycle management, and cloud service provid-ers want greater control over resource management. To support the sepa-ration of concerns and ease of use, a minimal-intrusive service delivery model is presented in Chap. 4. This model uses a CloudLightning-specific service description language, blueprinting, and gateway service to enable enterprise application developers to specify comprehensive constraints and quality of service parameters for services and/or resources and, based on the specified constraints and parameters, provide an optimal deployment of the resources.

Finally, Chap. 5 addresses the issue of validation of such a novel architecture. As per Sudeikat et al. (2009), the validation of self-organising models summatively and formatively presents significant challenges that are further complicated at hyperscale. Chapter 5 presents CloudLightning's work on the design and implementation of a Warehouse-Scale cloud simulator for validating the performance of CloudLightning.

1.9   CHAPTER 1 RELATED CLOUDLIGHTNING READINGS

1. Lynn, T., Xiong, H., Dong, D., Momani, B., Gravvanis, G. A., Filelis-Papadopoulos, et al. (2016, April). CLOUDLIGHTNING: A framework for a self-organising and self-managing heterogeneous Cloud. In *Proceedings of the 6th International Conference on Cloud Computing and Services Science (CLOSER 2016), 1 and 2* (pp. 333–338). SCITEPRESS-Science and Technology Publications, Lda.

2. Lynn, T., Kenny, D., & Gourinovitch, A. (2015). Global HPC market. Retrieved November 6, 2017, from https://cloudlightning. eu/?ddownload=2446

3. Lynn, T., Kenny, D., Gourinovitch, A., Persehais, A., Tierney, G., Duignam, M., et al. (2015). 3D image rendering. Retrieved November 6, 2017, from https://cloudlightning.eu/?ddownload=2435

4. Lynn, T., & Gourinovitch, A. (2016). Overview of the HPC market for genome sequence. Retrieved November 6, 2017, from https:// cloudlightning.eu/?ddownload=2443

5. Lynn, T., Gourinovitch, A., Kenny, D., & Liang, X. (2016). Drivers and barriers to using high performance computing in the cloud. Retrieved November 6, 2017, from https://cloudlightning. eu/?ddownload=2904

6. Callan, M., Gourinovitch, A., & Lynn, T. (2016). The Global Data Center market. Retrieved November 6, 2017, from https:// cloudlightning.eu/?ddownload=3588

NOTES

1. https://www.top500.org/green500/
2. There are other niche processor solutions worth exploring including Automata Processors for graph analysis, pattern matching, and data analytics; Digital Signal Processor for processing real-world analogue signals; Application-Specific Integrated Circuits (ASICs) for use cases such as bitcoin mining; and neuromorphic chips for cognitive computing. For more discussion, see Zahran (2017).

REFERENCES

Amazon Web Services. (2015). An introduction to high performance computing on AWS [White Paper]. Seattle, WA: Amazon Web Services. Retrieved October 23, 2017, from https://d0.awsstatic.com/whitepapers/Intro_to_HPC_on_AWS.pdf

Ashby, W. R. (1947). Principles of the self-organizing dynamic system. *The Journal of General Psychology, 37*(2), 125–128.

Awada, U., Li, K., & Shen, Y. (2014). Energy consumption in cloud computing data centres. *International Journal of Cloud Computing and Services Science, 3*(3), 145.

Barroso, L. A., & Hölzle, U. (2007). The case for energy-proportional computing. *Computer, 40*(12), 33–37.

Boston Consulting Group (2001). *A revolution in R&D—How genomics and genetics are transforming the bio-pharmaceutical industry*. Boston, MA: Boston Consulting Group. Retrieved October 23, 2017, from https://www.bcg.com/documents/file13745.pdf

Brandic, I. (2009, July). Towards self-manageable cloud services. In *Computer Software and Applications Conference, 2009. COMPSAC'09. 33rd Annual IEEE International*, Vol. 2 (pp. 128–133). IEEE.

Branke, J., Mnif, M., Muller-Schloer, C., & Prothmann, H. (2006, November). Organic computing—Addressing complexity by controlled self-organization. In *Second International Symposium on Leveraging Applications of Formal Methods, Verification and Validation, 2006 (ISoLA 2006)* (pp. 185–191). IEEE.

Chow, O. (2017). AWS & Intel: A partnership dedicated to cloud innovations [PowerPoint slides]. *SlideShare*. Retrieved October 23, 2017, from https://www.slideshare.net/AmazonWebServices/aws-intel-a-partnership-dedicated-to-cloud-innovations-77355517

Cisco. (2016). Cisco Global Cloud index: Forecast and methodology, 2015–2020 [White Paper]. *Cisco*. Retrieved October 23, 2017, from https://www.cisco.com/c/dam/en/us/solutions/collateral/service-provider/global-cloud-index-gci/white-paper-c11-738085.pdf

Clark, J. (2014, November 11). 5 numbers that illustrate the mind-bending size of Amazon's cloud. *Bloomberg*. Retrieved October 23, 2017, from https://www.bloomberg.com/news/2014-11-14/5-numbers-that-illustrate-the-mind-bending-size-of-amazon-s-cloud.html

Crago, S., Dunn, K., Eads, P., Hochstein, L., Kang, D. I., Kang, M., Modium, D., Singh, K., Suh, J., & Walters, J. P. (2011, September). Heterogeneous cloud computing. In *2011 IEEE International Conference on Cluster Computing (CLUSTER)* (pp. 378–385). IEEE.

Crago, S. P., & Walters, J. P. (2015). Heterogeneous cloud computing: The way forward. *Computer, 48*(1), 59–61.

Data Center Knowledge. (2017, March 16). Google Data Center FAQ. *Data Center Knowledge*. Retrieved October 23, 2017, from http://www.datacenterknowledge.com/archives/2017/03/16/google-data-center-faq

De Wolf, T., & Holvoet, T. (2004, July). Emergence versus self-organisation: Different concepts but promising when combined. In *International Workshop on Engineering Self-organising Applications* (pp. 1–15). Berlin: Springer.

Dobson, S., Sterritt, R., Nixon, P., & Hinchey, M. (2010). Fulfilling the vision of autonomic computing. *Computer, 43*(1), 35–41.

Dongarra, J. (2016, June 24). Report on the Sunway TaihuLight System. Retrieved November 7, 2017, from http://www.netlib.org/utk/people/JackDongarra/PAPERS/sunway-report-2016.pdf

Eijkhout, V., van de Geijn, R., & Chow, E. (2016). Introduction to high performance scientific computing. *Zenodo*. https://doi.org/10.5281/zenodo.49897

Elgar, T. (2010, December). Intel Many Integrated Core (MIC) architecture [PowerPoint Slides]. In *2nd UK GPU Computing Conference*, December 2010. Retrieved October 23, 2017, from http://www.many-core.group.cam.ac.uk/ukgpucc2/talks/Elgar.pdf

Esmaeilzadeh, H., Blem, E., St Amant, R., Sankaralingam, K., & Burger, D. (2011, June). Dark silicon and the end of multicore scaling. *ACM SIGARCH Computer Architecture News, 39*(3), 365–376. ACM.

Ezell, S. J., & Atkinson, R. D. (2016, April). *The vital importance of high-performance computing to US competitiveness*. Washington, DC: Information Technology and Innovation Foundation. Retrieved October 23, 2017, from http://www2.itif.org/2016-high-performance-computing.pdf

Feldman, M. (2016, June 20). China tops supercomputer rankings with new 93-Petaflop Machine. *TOP500.org*. Retrieved October 23, 2017, from https://www.top500.org/news/china-tops-supercomputer-rankings-with-new-93-petaflop-machine/

Ganek, A. G., & Corbi, T. A. (2003). The dawning of the autonomic computing era. *IBM Systems Journal, 42*(1), 5–18.

Garfinkel, S. (1999). *Architects of the information society: 35 years of the Laboratory for Computer Science at MIT*. MIT Press.

Gutierrez-Garcia, J. O., & Sim, K. M. (2010, November). Self-organizing agents for service composition in cloud computing. In *2010 IEEE Second International Conference on Cloud Computing Technology and Science (CloudCom)* (pp. 59–66). IEEE.

Herrmann, K., Muhl, G., & Geihs, K. (2005). Self management: The solution to complexity or just another problem? *IEEE Distributed Systems Online, 6*(1), 1.

Heylighen, F. (1989). Self-organization, emergence and the architecture of complexity. In *Proceedings of the 1st European Conference on System Science* (pp. 18, 23–32). Paris: AFCET.

Heylighen, F., & Gershenson, C. (2003). The meaning of self-organization in computing. *IEEE Intelligent Systems, 18*(4), 72–75.

Horn, P. (2001). Autonomic computing: IBM's perspective on the state of information technology. *IBM.* Retrieved October 23, 2017, from http://people. scs.carleton.ca/~soma/biosec/readings/autonomic_computing.pdf

IBM. (2005). An architectural blueprint for autonomic computing [White Paper]. *IBM.* Retrieved October 23, 2017, from https://www-03.ibm.com/autonomic/ pdfs/AC%20Blueprint%20White%20Paper%20V7.pdf

IDC. (2014). *Market analysis perspective: Worldwide HPC, 2014—Directions, trends, and customer requirements.* Framingham, MA.

IDC. (2015). *High performance computing in the EU: Progress on the implementation of the European HPC strategy.* Brussels, Belgium: European Commission.

Intersect360 Research. (2014). *Worldwide high performance computing 2013: Total market model and 2014–18 forecast.* Sunnyvale, CA.

Kephart, J. O., & Chess, D. M. (2003). The vision of autonomic computing. *Computer, 36*(1), 41–50.

Kim, W. (2009). Cloud computing: Today and tomorrow. *Journal of Object Technology, 8*(1), 65–72.

Kramer, J., & Magee, J. (2007, May). Self-managed systems: An architectural challenge. In *2007 Future of Software Engineering* (pp. 259–268). IEEE Computer Society.

Lewes, G. (1875). *Problems of life and mind* (Vol. 2). London, UK: Kegan, Paul, Trench, Turbner.

Li, J. F., Peng, J., Cao, X., & Li, H. Y. (2011). A task scheduling algorithm based on improved ant colony optimization in cloud computing environment. *Energy Procedia, 13*, 6833–6840.

Licklider, J. C. (1963). Memorandum for members and affiliates of the intergalactic computer network. *Advanced Research Projects Agency.* Washington, DC. Retrieved October 23, 2017, from http://www.kurzweilai.net/ memorandum-for-members-and-affiliates-of-the-intergalactic-computer-network

Mamei, M., & Zambonelli, F. (2003, July). Self-organization in multi agent systems: A middleware approach. In *International Workshop on Engineering Self-organising Applications* (pp. 233–248). Berlin: Springer.

Marinescu, D. (2017). *Complex systems and clouds—A self-organization and self-management perspective.* Cambridge, MA: Elsevier.

Marinescu, D. C., Paya, A., Morrison, J. P., & Healy, P. (2013, December 12). An auction-driven self-organizing cloud delivery model. Retrieved October 23, 2017, from arXiv preprint https://arxiv.org/abs/1312.2998 [cs.DC].

Mell, P., & Grance, T. (2011). *The NIST definition of cloud computing. Special Publication 800–145.* Gaithersburg, MD: National Institute of Standards and Technology.

Mergen, M. F., Uhlig, V., Krieger, O., & Xenidis, J. (2006). Virtualization for high-performance computing. *ACM SIGOPS Operating Systems Review, 40*(2), 8–11.

Müller-Schloer, C., Schmeck, H., & Ungerer, T. (Eds.). (2011). *Organic computing—A paradigm shift for complex systems.* Springer Science & Business Media.

Nami, M. R., Bertels, K., & Vassiliadis, S. (2006, November). Autonomic computing systems: Issues and challenges. In *17th Annual Workshop on Circuits, Systems and Signal Processing.*

National Supercomputing Centre, WuXi. (n.d.). Hardware. Retrieved October 23, 2017, from http://www.nsccwx.cn/wxcyw/soft1.php?word=soft&i=46

Nishant, K., Sharma, P., Krishna, V., Gupta, C., Singh, K. P., & Rastogi, R. (2012, March). Load balancing of nodes in cloud using ant colony optimization. In *2012 UKSim 14th International Conference on Computer Modelling and Simulation (UKSim)* (pp. 3–8). IEEE.

Owens, J. D., Luebke, D., Govindaraju, N., Harris, M., Krüger, J., Lefohn, A. E., et al. (2007, March). A survey of general-purpose computation on graphics hardware. *Computer Graphics Forum, 26*(1), 80–113. Blackwell Publishing.

Pandey, S., Wu, L., Guru, S. M., & Buyya, R. (2010, April). A particle swarm optimization-based heuristic for scheduling workflow applications in cloud computing environments. In *2010 24th IEEE International Conference on Advanced Information Networking and Applications (AINA)* (pp. 400–407). IEEE.

Papazoglou, M. P. (2012). Cloud blueprints for integrating and managing cloud federations. In *Software service and application engineering* (pp. 102–119). Berlin: Springer.

Parunak, H. V. D., & Brueckner, S. A. (2004). Engineering swarming systems. In *Methodologies and Software Engineering for Agent Systems* (pp. 341–376). Springer US.

Pell, O., & Mencer, O. (2011). Surviving the end of frequency scaling with reconfigurable dataflow computing. *ACM SIGARCH Computer Architecture News, 39*(4), 60–65.

Pell, O., Mencer, O., Tsoi, K. H., & Luk, W. (2013). Maximum performance computing with dataflow engines. In *High-performance computing using FPGAs* (pp. 747–774). New York: Springer.

Proaño, J., Carrión, C., & Caminero, M. B. (2014, April). An open-source framework for integrating heterogeneous resources in Private Clouds. In *4th International Conference on Cloud Computing and Services Science (CLOSER 2014)* (pp. 129–134). INSTICC.

Puviani, M., & Frei, R. (2013, October). Self-management for cloud computing. In *Science and Information Conference (SAI)* (pp. 940–946). IEEE.

Ray, J., Trebon, N., Armstrong, R. C., Shende, S., & Malony, A. (2004, April). Performance measurement and modeling of component applications in a high performance computing environment: A case study. In *Proceedings of 18th International Conference on Parallel and Distributed Processing Symposium, 2004* (p. 95), IEEE.

Rogers, P., & Fellow, A. C. (2013, August). Heterogeneous system architecture overview. *Hot Chips, 25.*

Schmeck, H. (2005, May). Organic computing—A new vision for distributed embedded systems. In *Eighth IEEE International Symposium on Object-oriented Real-time Distributed Computing, 2005 (ISORC 2005)* (pp. 201–203). IEEE.

Scogland, T. R., Steffen, C. P., Wilde, T., Parent, F., Coghlan, S., Bates, N., et al. (2014, March). A power-measurement methodology for large-scale, high-performance computing. In *Proceedings of the 5th ACM/SPEC International Conference on Performance Engineering* (pp. 149–159). ACM.

Serugendo, G. D. M., Gleizes, M. P., & Karageorgos, A. (2011). Self-organising systems. In *Self-organising software* (pp. 7–32). Berlin: Springer.

Severance, C., & Dowd, K. (2010). *High performance computing.* Houston, TX: Connexions.

Shan, A. (2006). Heterogeneous processing: A strategy for augmenting Moore's law. *Linux Journal, 142, 7.*

Shi, L., Chen, H., Sun, J., & Li, K. (2012). vCUDA: GPU-accelerated high-performance computing in virtual machines. *IEEE Transactions on Computers, 61*(6), 804–816.

Sudeikat, J., Braubach, L., Pokahr, A., Renz, W., & Lamersdorf, W. (2009). Systematically engineering self-organizing systems: The SodekoVS approach. *Electronic Communications of the EASST, 17.*

Teodoro, G., Kurc, T., Kong, J., Cooper, L., & Saltz, J. (2014, May). Comparative performance analysis of Intel (R) Xeon Phi (TM), GPU, and CPU: A case study from microscopy image analysis. In *Proceedings of 28th International Conference on Parallel and Distributed Processing Symposium, 2014 IEEE* (pp. 1063–1072). IEEE.

Trader, T. (2017, June 19). Top500 results: Latest list trends and what's in store. Retrieved November 7, 2017, from https://www.hpcwire.com/2017/06/19/49th-top500-list-announced-isc/

Turing, A. M. (1952). The chemical basis of morphogenesis. *Philosophical Transactions of the Royal Society of London B: Biological Sciences, 237*(641), 37–72.

Yeo, S., & Lee, H. H. (2011). Using mathematical modeling in provisioning a heterogeneous cloud computing environment. *Computer, 44*(8), 55–62.

Zahran, M. (2017). Heterogeneous computing: Here to stay. *Communications of the ACM, 60*(3), 42–45.

Zhang, Q., Cheng, L., & Boutaba, R. (2010). Cloud computing: State-of-the-art and research challenges. *Journal of Internet Services and Applications, 1*(1), 7–18.

CHAPTER 2

Cloud Architectures and Management Approaches

Dapeng Dong, Huanhuan Xiong, Gabriel G. Castañe, and John P. Morrison

Abstract An overview of the traditional three-layer cloud architecture is presented as background for motivating the transition to clouds containing heterogeneous resources. Whereas this transition adds many important features to the cloud, including improved service delivery and reduced energy consumption, it also results in a number of challenges associated with the efficient management of these new and diverse resources. The CloudLightning architecture is proposed as a candidate for addressing this emerging complexity, and a description of its components and their relationships is given.

Keywords Cloud architecture • Infrastructure • Management • Service delivery model • Heterogeneous cloud

D. Dong (✉) • H. Xiong • G. G. Castañe • J. P. Morrison
Department of Computer Science, University College Cork, Cork, Ireland
e-mail: d.dong@cs.ucc.ie; h.xiong@cs.ucc.ie; gabriel.gonzalezcastane@ucc.ie; j.morrison@cs.ucc.ie

© The Author(s) 2018   31
T. Lynn et al. (eds.), *Heterogeneity, High Performance Computing, Self-Organization and the Cloud*, Palgrave Studies in Digital Business & Enabling Technologies,
https://doi.org/10.1007/978-3-319-76038-4_2

2.1   Introduction

Cloud end-users are demanding greater performance and diversity of cloud services than ever before. As discussed in Chap. 1, the high-performance computing (HPC) and other end-user communities are seeking to exploit new and diverse hardware designed for specialist tasks. As well as supporting these new demands, cloud service providers (CSPs) face the challenges of achieving cost-effective scalability while increasing energy efficiency. Accommodating heterogeneity and maximising server utilisation (and by inference minimising over-provisioning) is a significant shift from conventional homogeneous cloud computing service design. This is particularly the case with HPC where end-users require a greater level of access and control over elements of the cloud infrastructure. To access heterogeneous resources, exploit these resources to reduce application development effort, make optimisation easier, and simplify service deployment, a re-evaluation of our approach to both resource management and service delivery is required.

The remainder of this chapter discusses conventional cloud architecture designs and provides an overview of the CloudLightning architecture, a novel architecture designed to meet the challenges of the heterogeneous cloud. The next section presents the three layers of conventional cloud architectures—the Infrastructure Layer, the Cloud Management Layer, and the Service Delivery Layer. This is followed by a discussion of the main challenges associated with transitioning to a truly heterogeneous cloud with an emphasis on resource management and abstraction. In Sect. 2.4 CloudLightning is presented, a cloud architecture inspired by the design principles of emergence, self-organisation, self-management, and the separation of concerns discussed in Chap. 1. Each functional component and their relationships are detailed to provide insights into how it differs from the conventional cloud and realises important properties from the end-user and CSP perspectives including support for heterogeneity, ease of use, auto-scaling, data locality, high availability (HA), and networking organisation.

2.2   Cloud Architecture

Over the last decade, large-scale consumer-facing cloud services have been created by service providers such as Amazon, Microsoft, Google, and Rackspace. These data centres are large industrial facilities containing the computing infrastructure that runs their services: servers, storage arrays, and networking equipment. This core equipment requires supporting infrastructure in the form of power, cooling, and external networking links. Reliable service delivery depends on the holistic management of all of this infrastructure as a single integrated entity. Architecturally, this holistic management can be logically separated into three layers from bottom to top including an Infrastructure Layer, a Cloud Management Layer, and a Service Delivery Layer, as shown in Fig. 2.1.

2.2.1   Infrastructure Organisation

Cloud infrastructure design is the art of balancing requirements to ensure data centre scalability, maintaining server fault tolerance, minimising costs, and maximising bisection end-to-end bandwidth (Kim 2011; Wang et al. 2014). Traditional data centre infrastructure is based on a hierarchical structure typically with a three-tier design including the Access Layer, the

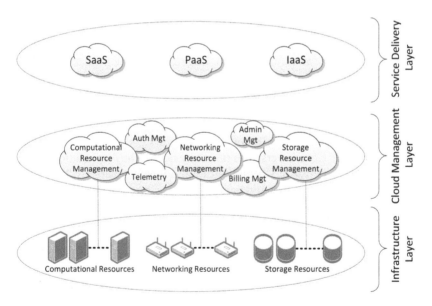

Fig. 2.1 Classical cloud architecture is considered to be composed of three layers. The Service Delivery Layer is one seen by users; this layer is realised by the Cloud Management Layer, which is also responsible for realising the objectives of the Cloud Service; the Infrastructure Layer comprises of the underlying collection of storage, computing, and network resources and their required hardware and software

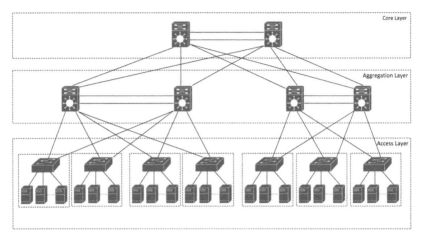

Fig. 2.2 The traditional three-tier networking infrastructure

Aggregation Layer, and the Core Layer (Martin Pueblas 2010), as shown in Fig. 2.2.

- *The Access Layer* (also called the Edge Layer): The primary function of the Access Layer is to connect servers that typically reside in the same rack. An Access-Layer switch is thus often referred to as a Top-of-Rack (ToR) switch.
- *The Aggregation Layer* (also called, the Distribution Layer): The Aggregation Layer is a multi-purpose system that interfaces the Access and Core Layers. The main function of the Aggregation Layer is to keep the various communication domains separately, thus providing intelligent switching and HA between regional ToRs.
- *The Core Layer*: The Core Layer is responsible for providing high-speed, scalable, and reliable connectivity across the entire data centre.

This traditional three-tier data centre design is created with simplicity in mind. The design relies on the use of high-end enterprise-class switches in the upper layers, whereas the lower layers can function effectively with less sophisticated equipment. Previous research has indicated that adding additional servers to a data centre, using the traditional three-tier design, will reduce the end-to-end bisection bandwidth in proportion to the size of the data centre (Al-Fares et al. 2008). In support of cloud computing and in response to the rise in popularity of Big Data and High-Performance Computing as a Service (BDaaS and HPCaaS, respectively), the organisation of the infrastructure in modern data centres is biased towards scalability and high throughput.

In general, design strategies are centred on two basic models—the Switch-Centric model and Server-Centric model. The next section discusses these models and the main network designs associated with these models.

2.2.1.1 The Switch-Centric Model

In the Switch-Centric model, servers are interconnected using switches and routers. The Fat-tree network is a representative of the Switch-Centric model that is widely acknowledged and used for data centre networking infrastructure. A Fat-tree network is also known as Clos topology (Leiserson 1985). In a Fat-tree network, servers are grouped into Points of Delivery (PoDs). A PoD consists of n number of servers and n number of switches. $n/2$ switches are connected to n servers and act as Access-Layer switches. The remaining switches are connected to the Access-Layer switches and, to each other, acting as Aggregation-Layer switches. Moreover, PoDs are connected using additional $(n/2)^2$ switches acting as Core-Level interconnections. Thus, the Fat-tree design guarantees a one-to-one over-subscription ratio between any pair of nodes in the network. However, the scalability of the infrastructure is limited by the number of ports available on each switch. BCube (Guo et al. 2009) is another Switch-Centric design based on a recursive-defined topology. In a BCube design, n servers are connected to an n-port switch forming a cell. n cells are connected through n switches to form a cube. BCube is designed for modular data centres and accommodates high performance in a multicast and broadcast network; however, the complexity of network cabling is relatively high. Portland (Niranjan Mysore et al. 2009), RBridges (Ghanwani 2011), SmartBridge (Rodeheffer 2000), SEATTLE (Kim 2011), and VL2 (Greenberg et al. 2011) are commonly used routing and forwarding protocols and network address schemes for the Fat-tree-based infrastructure.

2.2.1.2 The Server-Centric Model

In the Server-Centric model, both servers and switches participate in packet routing, and in the Server-Centric model, both servers and switches participate in packet routing and forwarding. DCell (Guo et al. 2008) is a representative implementation of the Server-Centric model. In DCell, n servers are connected to an n-port switch forming the smallest entity known as a Cell. $n+1$ number of Cells are interconnected via the network interfaces of each server, thus forming a larger network. The hierarchical topological design makes DCell networks scalable and robust. However, the network diameter increases exponentially with the size of the network. This implies that Cells in the inner layer will carry more network traffic, and end-to-end communications may experience greater latency. FlatNet (Lin et al. 2012) is another Server-Centric recursive-defined network. The FlatNet design uses more switches to achieve higher scalability, n^3, compared to n^2 of DCell. Based on similar rules used in DCell, FlatNet organises n servers in an n-port switch as a Cell. A higher layer is formed from n^2 number of lower layers. In FiConn configurations, the main network interfaces of a server are connected to their corresponding ToR switch(es), and the redundant network interfaces of a server is used to establish direct server-to-server connections (Li et al. 2009). In contrast to DCell, FiConn, and FlatNet, the SprintNet design focuses on high performance. SprintNet uses multiple, c number of switches connecting n servers in each Cell, in which $n/(c+1)$ ports connect to other Cells in the network. Infrastructure expansions are achieved by adding $c*n/(c+1)$ Cells each time. The SprintNet is specially designed for high-throughput infrastructure.

The current trend is towards using a Server-Centric design based on a recursively defined topology. From a cloud management perspective, the number of servers determines scalability, the number of switches affects the infrastructure cost and the energy efficiency, the number of links indicates the complexity of constructing the network, and the diameter of the network directly influences the network throughput (high-throughput networks will improve the service delivery experience, especially for Big Data and HPC and high-throughput computing (HTC) applications). HPC and HTC based on heterogeneous computational resources may have specific requirements on the types of switches, port numbers, and link capacity. Unfortunately, none of the existing design schemes can guarantee scalability, fault tolerance, high performance, and energy efficiency at the same time. To this end, a hybrid infrastructure organisation scheme using the combination of several interconnected topological designs may be required. For example, a combination of Fat-tree, BCube, and SprintNet may be capable of providing the required infrastructure. As a side effect, a hybrid design introduces further complexity that must be managed.

2.2.2   *The Cloud Management Layer*

Depending on the business goals, the technologies chosen to implement a cloud architecture varies from vendor to vendor. In principle, all cloud architecture implementations aim to realise quality attributes that most appropriately reflect the business goals of the CSP. In Chap. 1, cloud computing was defined, as per National Institute of Standards and Technology, as having five properties including on-demand self-service, broad network access, resource pooling, rapid elasticity, and measured service (Mell and Grance 2011). Technically, any data centre having those properties can be considered as a cloud. These properties can be realised by composing a set of commonly acknowledged functional components, as shown in Fig. 2.3. In principle, all cloud management platforms follow the same architectural design, but their implementations vary greatly. The following sections give a high-level overview of how two representative cloud management platforms, namely OpenStack and Google Kubernetes, implement the classical cloud architecture, based on virtualisation and containerisation technologies, respectively.

2.2.2.1   *OpenStack*

OpenStack (OpenStack, LLC 2017) is an open-source cloud platform designed to manage virtualised environments. Hypervisors are used to virtualise servers; various technologies including Virtual Local Area Networks,

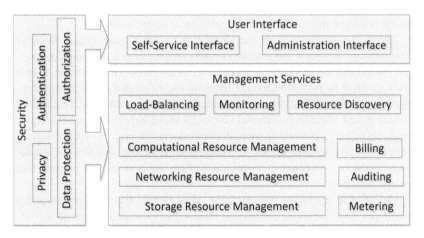

Fig. 2.3   Cloud management architect—a component view

Linux kernel namespaces, and various tunnelling techniques are used to virtualise networks; and storage resources are abstracted through the use of Network File Systems, Remote Volume, Object Storage, and other network-based clustering file systems such as GlusterFS (Red Hat & GlusterFS 2012), Ceph (Weil 2006), and Google File System (Ghemawat et al. 2003).

In particular, for managing computational resources, OpenStack uses a front-end Application Programming Interface (API) server for receiving and answering requests. Typically, allocating a computational resource will require other components, for example, a virtual network, a security group, and operating system images. This can be a complex task when dealing with multiple simultaneous requests with different configurations. In order to reduce this complexity, the front-end API server forwards the requests to a *nova-conductor* service. The *nova-conductor* coordinates various associated components to satisfy for a particular request. The *nova-conductor* uses a scheduler service (*nova-scheduler*) to locate potential physical server(s) that meet the specified requirements, including the number of Central Processing Unit (CPU) cores, the size of memory, and storage space. The requested resources (Virtual Machines [VMs]) will be deployed by a *nova-compute* service (by calling hypervisor-specific APIs) on the most appropriate physical servers. Architecturally, the computational resource management consists of a front-end API server, request coordinators (can be a group of resource coordinators to deal with high-volume requests), and an agent per computational node (executing the actual resource provisioning and deployment commands).

Managing networking in the cloud is a complex task. This is because conventional network functional components, for example, firewalls, routers, switches, networking connections, and Network Interface Cards (NICs), must be provided to end-users on top of shared physical networking resources and networking equipment. These cannot be virtualised or containerised like computational resources using hypervisors or container engines; rather, networking virtualisation is mainly built on top of several packet tagging/encapsulation techniques and the use of software implementations of respective networking devices such as virtual routers and virtual switches.

OpenStack storage systems are decoupled from computational resources. OpenStack offers several basic types of storage systems including traditional database systems, network-attached storage, and object storage. The back-end technologies supporting these storage systems vary greatly. In general, database systems and object storage are used by cloud applications, whereas remote volumes are used when creating VMs.

2.2.2.2 Google Kubernetes

Kubernetes is the most recent evolution of Google data centre management technology (Rensin 2015; Burns et al. 2016). Architecturally, Kubernetes uses a master/worker model. It consists of a master server and multiple minions (workers). The command line tools connect to the API endpoint in the master, which manages and orchestrates all minions. The minions receive instructions from the master and initialise local containers, appropriately.

A Kubernetes Master is composed of a number of components: the API server, the Replication Controller, the *etcd* Daemon, and the Scheduler. The API server is responsible for processing requests and for manipulating the underlying state objects. The Replication Controller determines how many pods or containers need to be run. The *etcd* Daemon stores configuration data. Lastly, the Scheduler is used to place work on an appropriate minion (or minions) based on an analysis of the state of the current infrastructure and the requirements of the service being provisioned.

A Kubernetes Minion is also composed of a number of components: the Kubelet, the Proxy, the cAdvisor, and a Pod. The Kubelet manages the lifecycle of containers in response to instructions from the master. The Proxy forwards network traffic to the appropriate containers. It performs primitive load balancing and is responsible for making sure that each networking environment is internally accessible while remaining isolated from other environments. The cAdvisor is a daemon that provides container users with an understanding of the resource usage and the performance characteristics of their containers. Finally, a Pod defines a collection of containers, deployed on the same minion, and provides them with a shared context.

2.2.3 The Service Delivery Layer

As outlined in Chap. 1, there are three basic cloud service delivery models: Software as a Service (SaaS), Platform as a Service (PaaS), and Infrastructure as a Service (IaaS). These service delivery models are also referred to as cloud business models or resource abstraction models. Each of these delivery models is realised in specific layers of the cloud architecture. IaaS, for example, provides end-users access to tangible physical infrastructures, such as physical servers, networking equipment, and storage systems. IaaS also provides access to virtualised physical servers, known as Virtual Machines. IaaS offers maximum flexibility to end-users for configuring and operating the acquired resources, thus IaaS targets end-user groups interested in building Information Technology (IT) infrastructure.

In order to reduce the configuration complexity and operational costs, CSPs can provide pre-configured platforms and offer those ready-to-use platforms to the end-user. This service model is often referred to as PaaS. Examples of PaaS are pre-configured operating systems (e.g., Linux, Windows), Web application servers (e.g., Apache Tomcat, Oracle Glassfish Red Hat JBoss), Workflow Engines (e.g., Apache Orchestration Director Engine), and Messaging frameworks (e.g., RabbitMQ, ZeroMQ). PaaS provides services to system administrators and developers in need of pre-configured platforms for their systems or applications to function as expected. Although PaaS can greatly reduce configuration complexity and operational costs, it still requires the end-users to have domain-specific knowledge to engage with the platforms being provided. There are also cloud end-users who are interested only in consuming services, such as email, business processes, customised applications, for example, Customer Relationship Management and Enterprise Resource Planning. When a CSP has installed, configured, and provided those customer-facing software solutions as a service, they are referred to as SaaS.

As the cloud ecosystem rapidly evolves, heterogeneous resources are being incorporated into the cloud environment, which has traditionally been homogeneous. This evolution requires multiple service abstraction modes to coexist and to be combined to provide more versatile services.

2.3   Transitioning to Heterogeneous Clouds

Cloud infrastructure has traditionally been built on homogeneous resources. This approach afforded simplicity of design and uniformity of resource management. In recent years, different types of resources have been made available to the cloud user community and have proven to be extremely popular due to their speed and modest power consumption. This evolution on the tradition design is thus leading to the emergence of the heterogeneous cloud. Heterogeneity is a broad concept. It can refer to different models of physical servers, produced by various manufacturers, and/or it can refer to different servers having different computational power, storage size, and networking capacities. Functionally, various types of coprocessors and accelerators, such as the Intel Xeon Phi Coprocessor

(Many Integrated Core [MIC]), the Field-Programmable Gate Array (FPGA), and the Graphical Processing Unit (GPU), have already been used in many production clouds. At a lower level, each type of CPU (Advanced Micro Devices, Intel, or even Advanced Reduced Instruction Set Computing Machine [ARM]), system memory (e.g., Double Data Rate {1, 2, 3}, 3D transistors), and storage types (e.g., mechanical disks and Solid State Disks) has different speeds and power consumption patterns. From a networking perspective, several types of networking connections (e.g., 1 Gb/s standard Ethernet, 10/40Gb/s high-speed Ethernet, Fibre Optical network, and InfiniBand) coexist in many major cloud deployments. The heterogeneity in hardware, resource organisation schemes, and software creates rich features and services that can support a wide range of applications from general web applications and networking infrastructure services to Big Data processing, high-performance/throughput computation applications, and recently the Network Virtual Function to support traditional telecommunication applications.

Heterogeneity also has its challenges from a cloud management perspective due to the complexity associated with managing diversity. Each type of hardware, resource organisation scheme, and software has its own unique static features, such as architecture, computation power, speed, and bandwidth, and each also exhibits different runtime patterns, such as power consumption, computation performance, access methods, and supporting software libraries. In order to efficiently and effectively manage such complex environments, the Cloud Management Layer must adapt to this evolving diversity. In this regard, the two most challenging aspects that must be addressed are the efficient management of resources and the support for flexible resource abstraction methods.

2.3.1   Resource Management

Heterogeneous resources introduce a large feature space into the cloud. The careful refinement of resource features and their combinations provide two clear advantages: (i) support for a wide range of applications and (ii) an appropriate mapping between application requirements/specifications and the resource features/characteristics. These can maximise the desires of both the end-user and the CSP, for example, respectively maximising application performance and reducing power consumption. This process requires resource management capable of efficiently and effectively manipulating such a large feature space at scale.

In the current cloud environment, resource scheduling can be catego-rised into three schemes including Monolithic, Two-Level Scheduling, and Shared-State (Schwarzkopf et al. 2013).

A Monolithic Scheduler has a single instance, is sequential, and must implement all policy choices in a single code base. The Google Borg scheduler is effectively monolithic, although the more recent releases of this scheduler have been optimised to provide internal parallelism and multi-threading to address HA and scalability. A Two-Level Scheduling approach separates application schedulers from resource schedulers. Mesos acts in this manner. It is an infrastructure management framework and makes use of a central master scheduler to decide how many resources from the available pool can be assigned to a framework. An application scheduler, within each framework, then allocates resources to applications within its own domain. Finally, a Shared-State scheme uses a Shared-State Scheduling approach, supporting multiple parallel schedulers. Each sched-uler is given a private, local, frequently updated copy of the global state for use in making local scheduling decisions. Once a scheduler makes a place-ment decision, it updates the shared copy of the global state in an atomic commit, and the time from state synchronisation to the commit attempt is called a transaction. Google Omega (Schwarzkopf et al. 2013; Burns et al. 2016) uses the Shared-State scheme. Omega schedulers operate in parallel using lock-free optimistic concurrency control. Omega is also designed to support multiple distinct workloads having their own application-specific interfaces, state machines, and scheduling policies.

Common cloud resource scheduling algorithms map applications to resources using resource availability metrics such as the number of avail-able CPU cores, the free memory, the available storage space, and other system-state information. These schedulers use as little information as pos-sible to make reasonable decisions in a timely manner. This approach is sufficient for a cloud composed of homogeneous resources. In contrast, heterogeneous clouds introduce a much higher degree of complexity for which conventional approaches to resource management are inadequate. Thus, new and innovative solutions are required to efficiently support the transition from the homogeneous to heterogeneous cloud.

2.3.2   Resource Abstraction

Current cloud management platforms are typically designed to manage either virtualised or containerised environments. Considering that the traditional cloud consists of homogeneous resources based on general-purpose processing units (CPU architectures) and standard hardware components, virtualisation and containerisation technologies have demonstrated their ability, in many production environments, to abstract standard hardware resources.

However, heterogeneity creates new challenges to existing resource abstraction methods. Specifically, many computation accelerators, such as MICs and GPUs, cannot be simply virtualised nor containerised without specific configurations being done at both the hardware and software levels. In particular, different models and manufacturers of the same type of computation accelerators may require different configurations on the host server (e.g., setting CPU features in the Basic Input/Output System and motherboard configurations) and in the software (e.g., changing kernel versions, updating operating system drivers, and choosing the appropriate hypervisor). This poses the challenge of how to flexibly use various resource abstraction methods to access different types of resources seamlessly.

2.4   THE CLOUDLIGHTNING APPROACH

The CloudLightning architecture has been constructed in an effort to address the challenges resulting from the transition to the emerging heterogeneous cloud. It recognises that the complexities associated with resource management due to this transition are nontrivial, and it proposes the use of self-organisation and self-management as a potential way forward. Thus, the architecture is composed of components and services with the necessary support for self-organisation and self-management. The CloudLightning architecture demonstrates how specialised hardware can be seamlessly integrated and the problems of centralised resource management at scale can be addressed, whilst recognising the inevitable added complexity resulting from supporting heterogeneity. Figure 2.4 shows the overview of the CloudLightning architecture, including the Service Delivery Layer, the Cloud Management Layer, and the Infrastructure Layer.

2.4.1   Infrastructure Organisation

The infrastructure organisation of CloudLightning is reminiscent of the Warehouse Scale Computer concept in which the infrastructure is composed

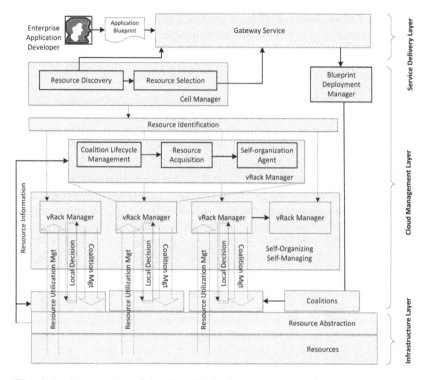

Fig. 2.4 An overview of the CloudLightning architecture showing how its various components are organised into the classical conceptual cloud layers

of *Cells*. A *Cell* is composed of Racks, which in turn contain servers of homogeneous hardware. In contrast, CloudLightning also incorporates heterogeneity by allowing different Racks to contain different computational resources.

2.4.2 Hardware Organisation

In a CloudLightning managed domain, physical servers are partitioned into groups based on geographical locations or regions; each of these partitions is called a *Cell*. A *Cell* is composed of a pool of heterogeneous computational resource, known as the Compute Resource Fabric. In the CloudLightning system, five elementary computational hardware types are considered explicitly. These include commodity servers (CPUs), servers with GPU accelerators, servers with MIC accelerators, servers with FPGA accelerators, and Non-uniform Memory Access Scale high-performance computer.

In a conventional data centre, physical racks are used to hold servers and switches. However, in a cloud deployment, the rack has no explicit identity that can be used to determine, from within the cloud software stack, where a particular compute/storage resource is physically located. To maintain information about groups of servers and to manage their resources, CloudLightning introduces virtual components called vRacks. A vRack contains a group of physical servers that share common properties including hardware type, hardware compatibility, and network connection type.

2.4.2.1 Resource Abstraction

The Hardware Abstraction Layer (HAL) provides a logical view of the underlying cloud infrastructure directly to the Cloud Management Layer. The HAL places resources into vRacks. Each vRack contains a certain number of homogeneous resources. The size of each vRack is initially determined by the management complexity for the type of resources to be managed. During the evolution of the system, a vRack may negotiate with other vRacks to exchange information and to transfer resources to achieve system goals such as maximising resource utilisation, reducing power consumption, and improving the service delivery experience.

When new hardware joins the CloudLightning managed domain, a dedicated Plug & Play interface is used to facilitate the connection of new hardware to the CloudLightning system. The newly connected hardware is required to expose available capacities and capabilities to the interface. In response, the interface will create CloudLightning-specific resources (CL-Resources) to represent the capabilities exposed. Depending on their type, these CL-Resources will be attached to an existing vRack, or if an appropriate vRack of this type is not available, a new vRack of an appropriate type is created. Where appropriate, the newly created vRack will be managed by a designated vRack Manager. This process is shown in Fig. 2.5.

2.4.3   The Cloud Management Layer

The CloudLightning management layer is shown in Fig. 2.4. The functional components and their relationships are explained in detail in the following sections.

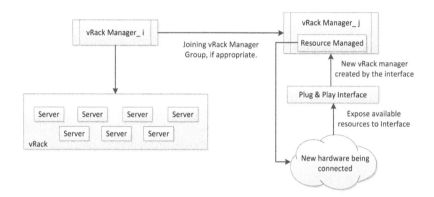

Fig. 2.5 Support for heterogeneous resources using Plug & Play interface at the Hardware Abstraction Layer

A Cell Manager is the software component associated with each Cell. The Cell Manager receives an *Application Requirements Document* from the Gateway Service, and it acquires CL-Resources in response to the requirements articulated in that "document". This can be done in at least one of two ways: either by allowing the user to select from a set of resources returned from a Resource Discovery phase or by allowing the system to assign appropriate resources immediately that meet the service requirements. In the former case, resource reservation is required while users make their choice, and in the latter case no reservation is needed.

2.4.3.1   CL-Resource Discovery

The CL-Resource Discovery process is initiated when the Cell Manager receives an *Application Requirements Document* from the Gateway. This "document" contains a set of Blueprint Requirements and a set of Service Requirements for each service in that Blueprint.

The function of the discovery process is to locate all of the possible CL-Resources that can be used to implement each of these services, consistent with particular constraints articulated in the list of Service Requirements.

The discovery process can determine information about dynamically changing capabilities and capacities by communicating with a group of vRack managers. From this information, the discovery process determines the CloudLightning system's ability to provide CL-Resources for each of the possible *Implementation Options* mentioned in the Service Requirements.

To guarantee these options remain available until the selection process is complete, all of the associated CL-Resources must be reserved by the associated vRack Managers. Thus, resources are potentially reserved across multiple vRack Managers until the selection process determines that they should be acquired or released. All of these *Implementation Options* are then passed directly to the CL-Resource selection process.

2.4.3.2   *The CL-Resource Selection*

This process applies the remaining constraints articulated in the list of *Service Requirements* and constraints associated with the *Blueprint Requirements* to determine a solution set consistent with all of the *Application Requirements*. If at this stage the solution set is not unique, the selection process will choose a unique solution by considering the options that minimise the overhead for the CSP. The associated CL-Resources in the solution set are then acquired automatically and those CL-Resources not in the solution set are released. Once the CL-Resources are acquired, their handlers are passed back to the Gateway for subsequent use by the Deployment Manager.

A vRack Manager is associated with each vRack. The function of a vRack Manager is to manage all of the CL-Resources that can be exposed from its associated vRack. In addition, it can create/aggregate CL-Resources in/on its vRack, as necessary. When the vRack Manager aggregates CL-Resources in its vRack, it creates a new type of CL-Resource called a *Coalition*. This is one of the defining characteristics of the CloudLightning system in that it allows CL-Resources to be formed into groups of homogeneous CL-Resource types to implement specific services with those requirements. A vRack Manager is responsible for managing the physical servers in its vRack. The set of servers associated with vRacks may be re-allocated over time. Similarly, new servers may be added to a Cell and others may be removed. This may trigger the creation/destruction/reorganisation of vRacks and their associated vRack Managers.

There are three functional components within each vRack Manager: a Resource Acquisition component, a Coalition Lifecycle Management component, and a Self-Organisation Agent.

2.4.3.3   *Resource Acquisition*

This component is activated by the selection process of the Cell Manager. It attempts to acquire CL-Resources; this can be guaranteed if they have been previously reserved. The CL-Resources being acquired may already exist within the vRack or they may have to be dynamically created by the vRack Manager. Once these CL-Resources have been acquired, their CL-Resource handlers are returned to the selection process of the Cell Manager.

2.4.3.4 Coalition Lifecycle Management

A Coalition is a special type of CL-Resource. In general, it represents a group of homogeneous CL-Resources, each of which exists within a single vRack. The vRack Manager may form a number of Coalitions, which may be persistent and used as a means of rapidly providing an implementation option for specific services. These persistent Coalitions are called *Static Coalitions*. The vRack Manager may also aggregate its CL-Resources, none of which may be a Coalition in itself, to form Coalitions dynamically in response to a specific CL-Resource acquisition request from Cell Manager. In managing dynamic CL-Resources, such as Coalitions, bin-packing strategies can be used to balance resource utilisation and power management. By appropriately managing the mix of static versus dynamic CL-Resources, faster service deployment can be balanced against potential savings on power consumption.

A Coalition is an entity that can be seen as an execution environment, formed by grouping together a number of CL-Resources. Coalitions may exist inside a single vRack and so each is under the control of single vRack Manager. The constituency of a Coalition may span multiple servers within that vRack. Coalitions are formed by a vRack Manager in response to specific service requirements. The vRack Manager may decide to persist Coalitions for improved service delivery, and these Coalitions are called Static Coalitions. Coalitions may also be formed dynamically by a vRack Manager again in response to specific service requirements. This dynamic formation may involve the dynamic creation of some or all of the constituent CL-Resources. When a dynamically formed Coalition is subsequently disbanded, its dynamically created constituents are destroyed, but any static CL-Resources used in its formation are left unchanged and persist to be reused in subsequent Coalition formations. Figure 2.6 illustrates a number of Coalitions in a vRack. From the illustration, it can be seen that a Coalition can exist entirely within a single server or can span multiple servers within the same vRack. In the situation that a single vRack Manager does not contain sufficient resources to satisfy a specific requirement, it may negotiate with an adjacent vRack Manager to acquire the appropriate resources.

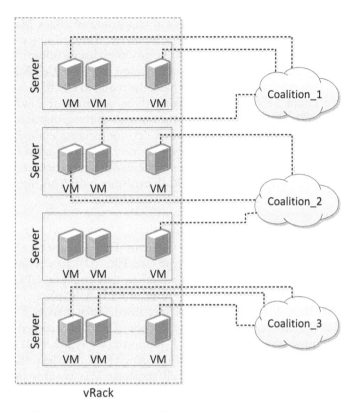

Fig. 2.6   Illustration of resource coalition

2.4.3.5   Self-Organisation Agent

The vRack Manager is a basic component of self-organisation in the CloudLightning system. vRack Managers organise themselves into groups and collectively determine local optimum strategies for CL-Resource management. The Self-Organisation Agent maintains information about other vRack Managers in the same group, it exchanges local state information with the Self-Organisation Agent in those vRack Managers, and it triggers power management decisions in the servers contained in its vRack. Negotiations between the various Self-Organising Agents within a vRack Manager group may result in the migration of servers from one vRack to another. Since CL-Resources may span multiple servers in the same vRack, any proposed migration must not violate the invariants associated with maintaining coalitions.

A vRack Manager Group is composed of a group of vRack Managers whose vRacks contain the same type of hardware. The Self-Organisation Agents of the vRack Managers within the group exchange information to optimally respond to resource discovery request from the Cell Manager. Together, they decide on if, and on where, the required CL-Resources are located or could be created. In making these decisions, the individual interests of each vRack Manager and the interests of the group as a whole are taken into account. This distributed decision process embodies the self-organisation strategy, which evolves to meet global objectives determined from the requirements driving the architecture design. vRack Managers are distinguished by the vRack hardware type. This distinction gives rise to a classification of the vRack Managers.

2.4.3.6 *Classification of vRack Managers*

Type-A vRack Managers are the most generic. They manage a collection of hardware resources of the same type (see Fig. 2.7). In one instance, these can be commodity hardware; in another, they could be CPU-GPU pairs, CPU-Data Flow Engine (DFE) pairs, or CPU-MIC pairs.

Type-B vRack Managers are more specialised. They manage a collection of HPC machines of the same type, each of which is exposed to the CloudLightning system as a single CL-Resource (see Fig. 2.8). If two or more HPC machines are managed by the same vRack Manager, then it is assumed that they are identical in all respects. This ensures that the CL-Resources exposed to the vRack Manager are the same.

Type-C vRack Managers manage a collection of hardware resources of the same type co-located on a high-speed interconnect (see Fig. 2.9). These can be commodity servers, or in other instances, they could be servers with GPU accelerators, servers with MIC accelerators, or servers with DFE accelerators.

Fig. 2.7 vRack Manager Type-A

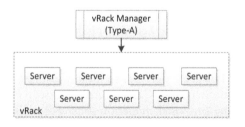

Fig. 2.8 vRack Manager Type-B

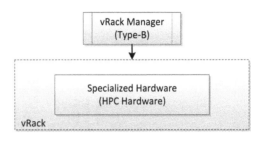

Fig. 2.9 vRack Manager Type-C

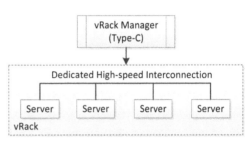

2.4.3.7 vRack Manager Activities

Type-A vRack Managers can only group with other Type-A managers (see Fig. 2.10). These groups can self-organise (e.g., in an attempt to improve power consumption). Self-organising involves servers migrating between vRack Managers in the same group. These groups also self-manage to improve service delivery but deciding locally which member of the group is the best to respond to particular service requests.

Neither Type-B nor Type-C vRack Managers engage in self-organisation. In general, the CL-Resources being managed are created from hardware of different types, thus cannot migrate to other vRack Managers. However, in principle, Type-B (see Fig. 2.11) vRack Managers can group together and Type-C (see Fig. 2.12) vRack Managers can group together in an effort to reduce the overall number of vRack Manager Groups. This in turn will simplify the administration required in the Cell Manager.

2.4.4   Service Delivery Model

The ready availability of large numbers of powerful, and increasingly het-erogeneous, resources being made available by CSPs is making possible the deployment of large, data, and compute-intensive, applications. In many cases, these, quite often legacy, applications are monolithic in construction

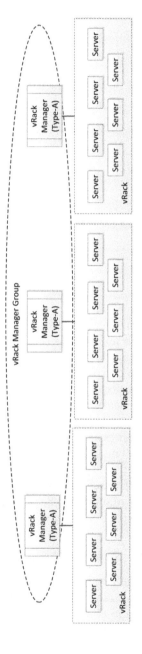

Fig. 2.10 vRack Manager Group Type-A

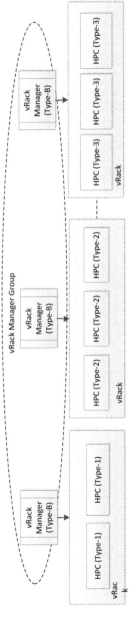

Fig. 2.11   vRack Manager Group Type-B

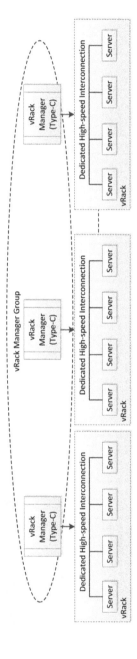

Fig. 2.12 vRack Manager Group Type-C

and require bespoke execution environments. Consequently, it can be challenging to deploy them in the cloud without acquiring IaaS and employing specialised engineering knowledge.

In this cloud usage model, the provider has no control over the effective utilisation of resources nor have cloud application developers an incentive to engage in costly customisation to increase resource efficiency when, regardless of the efficiency achieved, they are paying for the entire resource. Composing cloud services from workflows of large, possibly legacy, applications will most likely be the trend as support for emerging Big Data applications requires sophisticated, multi-phase data processing. Being essentially independent, the required resources for the applications that run in each of these phases may differ greatly in number and type, and hence the problems of cost and efficiency could be significantly exacerbated. Clearly, an approach is needed to allow the sophistication of the cloud to evolve in an efficient and cost-effective manner. It can be seen that there is no clear distinction between the concerns of cloud application developer and those of the Cloud Provider. The concerns of the CSP centre around efficient management and utilisation of cloud resources, and the concerns of cloud application developers centre on the specification, deployment, and service-level agreements (SLAs) associated with their applications.

To address this usability question, CloudLightning uses a Blueprint-oriented cloud application design and deployment approach. In this context, Blueprints are workflows in which nodes (*Service Element*) represent extant applications and edges distinguish the phases of the Blueprint execution where particular applications are active. All *Service Elements* are stored in a *Service Catalogue*, which is managed by the Gateway Service (Fig. 2.4). Cloud application developers may choose Service Elements from the *Service Catalogue* and link *Service Elements* to realise desired business logics. Attributes and parameters can be specified on a per *Service Element* basis. Altogether, the *Service Elements*, their linkages, and associated attributes and parameters comprise the application Blueprint, as shown in Fig. 2.13. The use of the Blueprint would drastically alter the current cloud usage model in that it would shift the burden of resource discovery, provisioning, and deployment from the cloud application developers to CSPs. This shift would greatly reduce the cost to, and the level of expertise needed by, cloud application developer while simultaneously giving CSPs full control over, and affording opportunities for the efficient use of, the cloud resources.

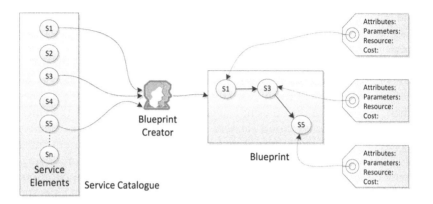

Fig. 2.13   CloudLightning Blueprint

2.4.5   Advanced Architecture Support

The design philosophy of the CloudLightning architecture is fundamentally different from the current cloud in operation. This results in the CloudLightning having different strategies for realising various important properties including auto-scaling, data locality, HA, and networking organisation.

2.4.5.1 Auto-Scaling

Scalability is one of the most important features in cloud computing. The CloudLightning system supports scalability provided that Blueprint developers explicitly indicate in the Blueprint which services are expected to require scaling. This explicit indication can be given by enclosing the services to be scaled within a *Scaling Envelope*. This envelope embeds services into Blueprint in order to monitor its load. When a pre-defined load threshold is crossed, this system service will dynamically acquire the appropriate resources from the CloudLightning system to scale the user service appropriately. By using the envelope in the Blueprint, consumers can see that execution of that Blueprint may result in charges relating to extra resources that cannot be determined statically. Additionally, the CloudLightning auto-scaling scheme allows application developers to explicitly specify how to service elasticity and partition data in a fine-grained manner. The scaling envelope and its associated impact on the CloudLightning system are illustrated in Fig. 2.14.

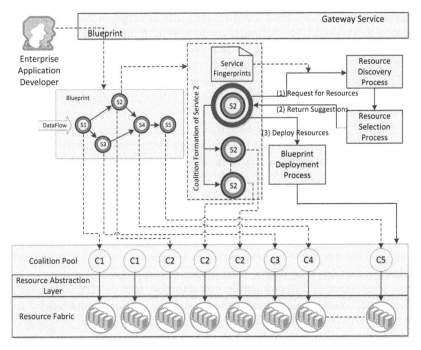

Fig. 2.14   Auto-scaling using CL Envelope Mechanism

2.4.5.2 *High Availability*

HA refers to the mechanisms used to ensure continuity of service delivery. If an infrastructure component (e.g., network equipment or server) fails, redundancy and flexible load balancing mechanisms may be employed to ensure that the overall service remains available. HA will be addressed within the CloudLightning system by using a Hot-Standby server for each of its software components. To provide HA of the services running on the CloudLightning system, service replication may be used. Since replication has an associated cost, the decision to use it should be made by the Blueprint developers by expressing that preference in the Blueprint. An envelope mechanism similar to the one used for auto-scaling may be used.

2.4.5.3 *Data Locality*

Data locality, defined as keeping data close to the computation, is one of the most important factors considered for HPC/HTC and Big Data applications. In the cloud environment, the concept of data locality is not well defined. The CloudLightning system does not propose to introduce mechanisms to give Blueprint developers control over the data locality, unless that control is provided explicitly by specialised CL-Resources dedicated to high-speed data processing. Thus, this functionality would have to be exposed to the Blueprint developers at the Blueprint level.

In the CloudLightning system, data locality constraints may have to be considered at various levels in the self-managed and self-organised components; thus, it may be necessary to develop strategies for data locality at the Coalition, vRack, and Cell level. For instance, if a given Blueprint consists of two services: Service_A and Service_B, knowing that if Service_A will generate significant amount of data that will be further processed by Service_B (this information will be specified between Service_A/B in the Blueprint specification), then this information is a potential data locality requirement for the Blueprint which will be thereafter used by Cloud Management Layer to deploy the Blueprint on appropriate resources. On the other hand, in different application domains, such as HPC/HTC and Big Data, many applications require local storage for computation. In cases where data locality is a predominant concern, CloudLightning system is designed to use Network Attached Storages (NAS) through high bandwidth links in order to minimise the data transmission cost over the network. However, in cases where the NAS is not present, local persistent storage can also be used.

2.4.5.4 Dynamic VPN Creation for Blueprint Service Execution

To create an isolated execution environment for each Blueprint, the CloudLightning Management Layer creates dedicated Virtual Private Networks (VPNs) for each Blueprint, as shown in Fig. 2.15. The services within a Blueprint need to communicate with each other, services are mapped onto dedicated Coalitions, which may be running on different physical servers. In addition, the Coalitions running various services of a Blueprint may extend over multiple vRacks. Regardless of their physical location in the CloudLightning system, dedicated VPNs created for each Blueprint will ensure that CL-Resources and the data exchange between them remain secure and private to the Blueprint from which they are constructed.

Fig. 2.15 Blueprint-driven VPN creation

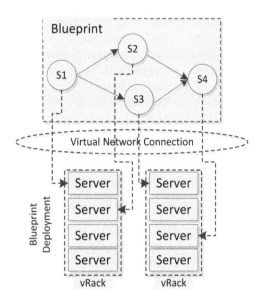

2.5 CONCLUSION

The trend for hardware vendors to create more specialised offerings, capable of providing faster, more accurate, and power-efficient solutions, looks set to continue. The increasing demand for this hardware and for access to HPC is driving an evolution of cloud computing that offers versatile services. A heterogeneous cloud at scale embodies many hardware types, each with different cost/performance/power profiles. This, together with the attempt to satisfy the disparate needs of a large and varied customer community, makes the heterogeneous cloud a complex system. In evolving to heterogeneous clouds, CSPs may no longer offer Software/Platform/Infrastructure as a service, separately. Instead, CSPs may undertake to offer a combination of these to the customer on demand. This approach would require a service orchestration designer tool that could be used to compose a set of services together with an appropriate expression of service-level requirements into a cloud application Blueprint. From this perspective, customers no longer need to be concerned about how solutions are provided; rather customers can concentrate on describing the problem to be solved. This also gives more control to the CSP over how to provision and optimise resources, to meet both consumer needs and system requirements. However, the complexity of managing resources in a heterogeneous cloud environment should not be underestimated. Self-organisation is one of the tools that can be employed to effectively address this complexity. More specifically, in a properly designed self-organising approach, global system objectives may be met as the by-product of emergent behaviour resulting from the application of low-level self-organising rules and strategies; this approach has been adopted by the CloudLightning project. In the next chapter, the self-organising and self-managing approach for cloud management in the CloudLightning architecture level and details for developing effective cloud organisation strategies and efficient resource management algorithms are addressed.

2.6   Chapter 2 Related CloudLightning Readings

1. Xiong, H., Dong, D., Filelis-Papadopoulos, C., Castané, G. G., Lynn, T., Marinescu, D. C., et al. (2017). CloudLightning: A self-organized self-managed heterogeneous cloud. *Annals of Computer Science and Information Systems, 11*, 749–758.

References

Al-Fares, M., Loukissas, A., & Vahdat, A. (2008). A scalable, commodity data center network architecture. *SIGCOMM Computer Communication Review, 38*(4), 63–74.

Burns, B., Grant, B., Oppenheimer, D., Brewer, E., & Wilkes, J. (2016). Borg, omega, and kubernetes. *Communications of the ACM, 59*(5), 50–57.

Ghanwani, R. P. (2011). *Routing Bridges (RBridges): Base protocol specification.* Internet Requests for Comments. RFC Editor.

Ghemawat, S., Gobioff, H., & Leung, S.-T. (2003). The Google File system. *SIGOPS Operating System Review, 37*(5), 29–43.

Greenberg, A., et al. (2011). VL2: A scalable and flexible data center network. *Communications of the ACM, 54*(3), 95–104.

Guo, C., et al. (2008). Dcell: A scalable and fault-tolerant network structure for data centers. *SIGCOMM Computer Communication Review, 38*(4), 75–86.

Guo, C., et al. (2009). BCube: A high performance, server-centric network architecture for modular data centers. *SIGCOMM Computer Communication Review, 39*(4), 63–74.

Kim, C., et al. (2011). SEATTLE: A scalable ethernet architecture for large enterprises. *ACM Transactions on Computer Systems, 29*(1), 1.

Leiserson, C. (1985). Fat-trees: Universal networks for hardware-efficient supercomputing. *IEEE Transactions on Computers, C-34*, 892–901.

Li, D., Guo, C., Wu, H., Tan, K., & Zhang, Y. (2009). FiConn: Using backup port for server interconnection in data centers. In *INFOCOM 2009* (pp. 2276–2285). IEEE.

Lin, D., Liu, Y., Hamdi, M., & Muppala, J. (2012). FlatNet: Towards a flatter data center network. In *Proceedings of Global Communications Conference (GLOBECOM)* (pp. 2499–2504). IEEE.

Martin Pueblas, B. C. (2010). *Cisco service ready architecture for schools design guide*. Cisco Systems, Inc.

Mell, P., & Grance, T. (2011). *The NIST definition of cloud computing*. Computer Security Division, Information Technology Laboratory, National Institute of Standards and Technology.

Niranjan Mysore, R., et al. (2009). PortLand: A scalable fault-tolerant layer 2 data center network fabric. *SIGCOMM Computer Communication Review, 39*(4), 39–50.

OpenStack, LLC. (2017). The openstack project. Retrieved from https://www.openstack.org

Red Hat & GlusterFS. (2012). *GlusterFS*. Retrieved from http://www.gluster.org

Rensin, D. K. (2015). *Kubernetes—Scheduling the future at Cloud Scale*. Sebastopol, CA: OSCON.

Rodeheffer, T. L. (2000). SmartBridge: A scalable bridge architecture. *SIGCOMM Computer Communication Review, 30*(4), 205–216.

Schwarzkopf, M. et al. (2013). Omega: Flexible, scalable schedulers for large compute clusters. In *Proceedings of the 8th ACM European Conference on Computer Systems* (pp. 351–364). ACM.

Wang, T., Zhiyang, S., Yu, X., & Hamdi, M. (2014). Rethinking the data center networking: Architecture, network protocols, and resource sharing. *Access, IEEE, 2*, 1481–1496.

Weil, S. A. (2006). Ceph: A scalable, high-performance distributed file system. In *Proceedings of the 7th symposium on Operating Systems Design and Implementation* (pp. 307–320). USENIX Association.

CHAPTER 3

Self-Organising, Self-Managing Frameworks and Strategies

Huanhuan Xiong, Christos Filelis-Papadopoulos,
Gabriel G. Castañe, Dapeng Dong, and John P. Morrison

Abstract A novel, general framework that can be used for constructing a self-organising and self-managing system is introduced. This framework is independent of the application domain. It embodies directed evolution, can be parameterised with different strategies, and supports both local and global goals. This framework is then used to apply the principles of self-organisation and self-management to resource management within the CloudLightning architecture.

Keywords Directed evolution • Self-organisation • Self-management • Strategies • Goal state

H. Xiong (✉) • G. G. Castañe • D. Dong • J. P. Morrison
Department of Computer Science, University College Cork, Cork, Ireland
e-mail: h.xiong@cs.ucc.ie; gabriel.gonzalezcastane@ucc.ie; d.dong@cs.ucc.ie; j.morrison@cs.ucc.ie

C. Filelis-Papadopoulos
Democritus University of Thrace, Komotini, Greece
e-mail: cpapad@ee.duth.gr

© The Author(s) 2018
T. Lynn et al. (eds.), *Heterogeneity, High Performance Computing, Self-Organization and the Cloud*, Palgrave Studies in Digital Business & Enabling Technologies,
https://doi.org/10.1007/978-3-319-76038-4_3

3.1   INTRODUCTION

A general framework for self-organisation and self-management (SOSM) is needed to support hierarchical architectures composed of autonomous components such as those described in the CloudLightning (CL) architecture discussed in Chap. 2. This chapter introduces a novel framework for SOSM developed to support CloudLightning. The next section presents key concepts in SOSM and how they are used to augment the CloudLightning architecture. The various SOSM mechanisms that enable components within CloudLightning to communicate, modify behaviour, make decisions, and cooperate with each other are then presented. Components may use different strategies for SOSM. As such, exemplar strategies are presented and illustrated in the context of CloudLightning through example scenarios.

3.2   KEY CONCEPTS

As discussed in Chap. 2 and mentioned above, the CloudLightning architecture is composed of autonomous components. Each component is equipped with various Strategies. These can be self-managing and/or self-organising strategies, and define how components at various levels in the hierarchy should evolve towards some ideal state known as the component's local goal.

In general, decisions being made by components at a particular level in the hierarchy can directly influence evolution in the adjacent levels. These influences may come from the top down, or from the bottom up. When coming from an upper level in the hierarchy, the process is called Directed Evolution. Directed Evolution signals the desire of the upper level to have the components, in the level underneath, change in operation or in configuration, to align with the goal of the upper level. Since components at a particular level also have local goals, the overall evolution that is brought about at that level should respect progress towards those local goals, while simultaneously accommodating the Impetus associated with the Directed Evolution process. An Impetus is communicated in the form of a tuple of values (i.e., a vector), known as a Weight. In a similar manner, a lower level in the hierarchy may directly influence the level above. This can be seen as Feedback from the lower level. This Feedback, in the form of tuples of values (i.e., vectors), known as Metrics, is derived from the operations of the components at the lower level and gives the upper level a Perception of how the lower layer is changing and evolving. Perceptions can be used to determine subsequent Directed Evolution decisions.

As part of the self-organisation process, the interaction of two or more components, in any level of the hierarchy, may result in component creation, component destruction, component splitting, and/or component merging.

A measure of how close a component is to stasis, and hence how suitable its operating characteristics are for contributing to the global goal, is referred to as its Suitability Index (SI). In principle, any component subject to Impetus and possessing a Perception has an associated SI. Thus, in the CloudLightning framework, the goal state of those components, and the global goal of the systems, can be cast in terms of maximising the respective SIs.

In summary, the CloudLightning framework defines a number of mechanisms as follows:

- A mechanism to communicate Impetus, through the transmission of weights, from a level in the hierarchy to the level below. This mechanism allows a component, higher in the hierarchy, to steer the evolution of components immediately below them in the hierarchy.
- A mechanism to allow components to communicate Feedback, through the transmission of metrics, to components in the next level up in the hierarchy.
- A mechanism to modify the behaviour of components in response to Impetus and Feedback.
- Mechanisms to allow components to make decisions in accordance with various strategies to maximise their individual SIs.
- Mechanisms to allow components at the same level in the hierarchy to cooperate with each other in accordance with various strategies to maximise collective and/or individual SIs.

All of these concepts, and their interactions, are visualised in Fig. 3.1.

The CloudLightning framework provides these mechanisms to enable the SOSM strategies being deployed and performed by individual components to move nearer to their goal state. Within this framework, each component can make local decisions in accordance with various SOSM strategies based on its current state (from the feedback loops) and imposed Impetus (from the directed evolution processes), maximising its SI. Overall, self-management is implemented at a system level, allowing the whole system to evolving towards its business/system objectives.

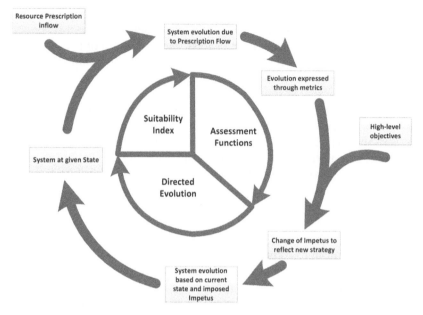

Fig. 3.1   Directed Evolution

3.3   Augmenting the CloudLightning Architecture

The CloudLightning architecture is initially augmented to include explicit entry points to the vRack Manager Groups. It can be seen from previous Chapter that these groups partition the resource space into different types of CL-Resources. This partitioning speeds up resource selection, since at most one CL-Resource type can be returned by the CloudLightning system for each service. The entry points into the differently typed vRack Manager Groups add an additional component to the CloudLightning architecture. Because of its routing characteristics described above, this component is called a pRouter. Figure 3.2 depicts this component in the augmented architecture.

From Fig. 3.2, it can be seen that there is an entry point into each vRack Manager Group, of the same CL-Resource type, hanging from each pRouter. These partition the space into smaller sets of CL-Resources of the same type. These entry points add yet another component to the

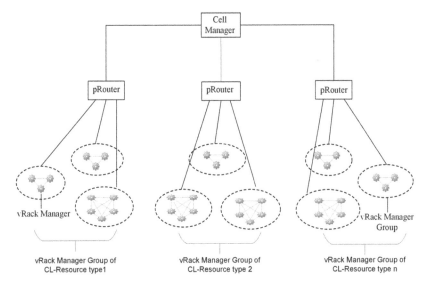

Fig. 3.2 Augmented CloudLightning architecture to include pRouters

CloudLightning architecture. Because this component connects all vRack Managers in the same group, it acts as a switch and is called a pSwitch. Figure 3.3 depicts this component in the augmented architecture.

It can be seen that the final augmented architecture forms a tree structure in which the root node corresponds to the Cell. The children of the Cell are pRouters, and there is at least one pRouter for each distinct CL-Resource type. The children of a pRouter are pSwitches. pSwitches partition the Virtual Rack Managers (vRMs), managing the same CL-Resource type, into groups. The number of pSwitches per pRouter is not fixed over time, neither is the size of the vRM groups managed by each pSwitch. In the following sections and chapters of this deliverable, it will be seen that pSwitches and vRMs can self-organise within groups, which are called Cooperatives, to emphasise their self-organising nature. To prohibit the creation of Cooperatives with different CL-Resource types, pSwitch Cooperatives cannot span pRouters. Similarly, to minimise administrative overhead and to simplify coalition formation, vRM Cooperatives (formerly called vRack Manager Groups) cannot span pSwitches.

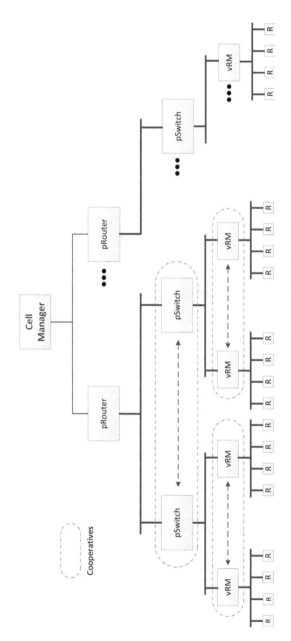

Fig. 3.3 Final augmented CloudLightning architecture illustrating its hierarchical nature with pRouter and pSwitch components

As the CloudLightning system evolves, it is anticipated that the number of pSwitches connected to a pRouter will change and will converge to some optimal number with respect to the global goal. This goal is derived from the Directed Evolution coming from the pRouter and from the pSwitch's efforts to achieve its local goal state. As part of the self-organisation process, pSwitches can be created, destroyed, merged, and split. In addition, pSwitches, within the same Cooperative, may exchange vRMs to optimise management. Together, the pRouters and the pSwitches form a reconfigurable and self-optimising switching fabric.

Similarly, it is anticipated that the number of vRMs connected to a pSwitch will change and will converge to some optimal number derived from the Directed Evolution coming from the pSwitch and from the vRM's efforts to achieve its local goal state. As part of the self-organisation process, vRMs can be created, destroyed, merged, and split. In addition, vRMs, within the same Cooperative, may exchange CL-Resources in an effort to maximise CL-Resource utilisation, minimise energy consumption, and facilitate coalition formation and management optimisation.

An important driving force behind the evolution of the CloudLightning system is the sequence of services/tasks that the system is required to execute. From the previous chapter, it can be seen that the process of maintaining a separation between resource and service life-cycles involves using the CloudLightning system to autonomously locate appropriate resources to execute each specific service/task. As part of this process, a description of these resources is passed to the CloudLightning system in an attempt to match appropriate resources with the service/task request. The term resource prescription (subsequently referred to simply as prescription) is introduced to refer to this description, and hence the pRouter is a prescription Router and the pSwitch is a prescription Switch.

vRMs form the lowest software level in the hierarchical organisation of the CloudLightning system. The next level up in this hierarchy is formed by grouping vRMs of the same type into Cooperatives. The elements of the Cooperatives, that is, its vRMs, self-organise by exchanging CL-Resources appropriately, to enable optimal management. Similarly, the elements of the pSwitch level self-organise by exchanging vRMs appropriately to enable optimal management. Finally, the elements of the pRouter level, that is, groups of pSwitches, self-organise by exchanging pSwitches appropriately to enable optimal management. All of these self-organising actions take place simultaneously resulting in the emergence of pathways through the hierarchy designed to optimise the ongoing propagation of resource prescriptions through the system.

3.4   SELF-ORGANISATION AND SELF-MANAGEMENT IN CLOUDLIGHTNING ARCHITECTURE

The general SOSM framework is mapped to the augmented hierarchical CloudLightning architecture outlined in the previous chapter. In the CloudLightning architecture, the autonomous components are the Cell, the pRouters, the pSwitches, and the vRMs. This framework provides Directed Evolution, self-management, and self-organisation mechanisms.

3.4.1   Directed Evolution

Directed Evolution is a mechanism to communicate a changing force throughout the system in a manner which effectively allows a component, higher in the hierarchy, to steer the evolution of the components immediately below them.

3.4.1.1 The Goal State

The goal of each component at all levels in the hierarchy is to maximise its SI.

The SI, η, is defined to be a combination of the Impetus and Perception expressed through a function $\eta\left(\vec{P}, \vec{I}\right)$, such that $\vec{I} \in R^N$, $\vec{P} \in R^N \rightarrow \eta\left(\vec{I}, \vec{P}\right) \in R$, where N is the number of parameters used to express Impetus and Perception.

Note that, in the Cell the SI is calculated per resource type.

The goal state for the pRouter and the pSwitch is:

$$\arg\max \eta\left(\vec{I}\left(\vec{w}\right), \vec{P}\left(\vec{m}\right)\right), \vec{w}, \vec{m} \in R^N \tag{3.1}$$

where $\vec{w}$ is an N-dimensional vector of weights corresponding to the Impetus and $\vec{m}$ is an N-dimensional vector of metrics obtained from the lower levels. Equivalently the goal state for the vRM is:

$$\arg\max \eta\left(\vec{I}\left(\vec{w}\right), \vec{P}\left(\vec{d}\right)\right), \vec{w}, \vec{d} \in R^N \tag{3.2}$$

where $\vec{w}$ is an N-dimensional vector of weights corresponding to the Impetus and $\vec{d}$ is an M-dimensional vector of metrics obtained from the Telemetry service.

3.4.1.2 Cell State

The Cell state is a set of vector tuples and function tuples of the form:

$$\{\{(\vec{w}, \vec{m}_1), (\vec{\mu}_1, \vec{\varphi}_1)\}, \{(\vec{w}, \vec{m}_2), (\vec{\mu}_2, \vec{\varphi}_2)\}, \ldots, \{(\vec{w}, \vec{m}_n), (\vec{\mu}_n, \vec{\varphi}_n)\}\} \qquad (3.3)$$

where n is the number of different pRouter types and $\vec{w}$ is the weight calculated by the Cell to effect steering. The tuple $(\vec{w}, \vec{m}_1)$ represents metrics and weights of the i-th pRouter, respectively, where $\vec{w} \in R^N$, $\vec{m}_i \in R^N$. The function tuple $(\vec{\mu}_i, \vec{\varphi}_i)$ is used to calculate the Impetus and Perception vectors, respectively, for each CL-Resource type maintained by each pRouter.

Since the Cell is at the highest level in the hierarchy, weights may be determined by the flow of tasks into the system and/or by local decisions made in an effort to move towards an objective goal state.

3.4.1.3 pRouter State and pSwitch State

The pRouter and pSwitch states can be described as a vector tuple $(\vec{w}, \vec{m})$, representing weights and metrics where $\vec{w} \in R^N$, $\vec{m} \in R^N$, and a function tuple $(\vec{\mu}, \vec{\varphi})$ is used to calculate Impetus and Perception, respectively.

3.4.1.4 vRM State

vRM state can be described as a vector tuple $(\vec{w}, \vec{d})$, representing weights and metrics where $\vec{w} \in R^N$, $\vec{d} \in R^N$, and a function tuple $(\vec{\mu}, \vec{\varphi})$ is used to calculate Impetus and Perception, respectively.

3.4.1.5 Steering by the Cell

There are at least two mechanisms for specifying a global goal state, G. The first is an objective goal specified to meet a specific business case. This can be set in a Cell, and in conjunction with the current local state of that Cell, adjustments can be made to the weights and applied to the underlying pRouters to steer them in that direction. By responding to this Impetus appropriately, the system will tend towards the goal state:

$$\vec{I}_{Cell} = \mu\left(\vec{I}'_{Cell}, \vec{G}_{Cell}, T_i\right) \qquad (3.4)$$

where $\vec{I}'_{Cell}$ is the current Impetus of the Cell, $\vec{I}_{Cell}$ is the new Impetus of the Cell, $\vec{G}_{Cell}$ is the goal state of the Cell, and T_i are resource prescriptions.

Alternatively, the global goal state of the system can be expressed as a maximisation of the local goal state of the Cell. That is:

$$\arg\max \eta_i\left(\vec{I}, \vec{P}\right),\ i = 1,\ \dots,\ n,\ \vec{I},\ \vec{P} \in R^N \tag{3.5}$$

where η_i is the suitability of i-th pRouter attached to the Cell.

3.4.1.6 Steering by the pRouter

Steering by a pRouter is a mechanism for calculating and transmitting an Impetus to its attached pSwitches:

Impetus is a function such that:

$$\vec{I}_{pRouter} = \mu\left(\vec{I}'_{pRouter}, \vec{I}_{Cell}\right),\ \vec{I}'_{pRouter} \in R^N,\ \vec{I}_{Cell} \in R^N \tag{3.6}$$

where $\vec{I}'_{pRouter}$ is the previous Impetus of the pRouter. Here $\vec{I}_{Cell}$ represents the weight coming from the Cell.

3.4.1.7 Steering by the pSwitch

Steering by a pSwitch is a mechanism for calculating and transmitting an Impetus to its attached vRMs:

$$\vec{I}_{pSwitch} = \mu\left(\vec{I}'_{pSwitch}, \vec{I}_{pRouter}\right),\ \vec{I}'_{pSwitch} \in R^N,\ \vec{I}_{pRouter} \in R^N \tag{3.7}$$

where $\vec{I}'_{pSwitch}$ is the previous Impetus of the pSwitch. Here $\vec{I}_{pRouter}$ represents the weight coming from the pRouter.

3.4.2 Self-Management Mechanisms

The self-managing components in the system include (a) pRouters and pSwitches, managing prescription routing, metrics, and weights; and (b) vRMs, managing task execution, metrics, weights, and CL-Resources.

3.4.2.1 Mechanism to Send Metrics from a vRM to pSwitch

A separate assessment function corresponding to one of N metrics is executed in each vRM, and the result is passed as an N-dimensional vector to the respective pSwitch associated with that vRM.

3.4.2.2 Mechanism to Send Metrics from a pSwitch to pRouter

A number of N-dimensional vectors will arrive at a pSwitch (one from each vRM in the cooperative defined by that pSwitch), and each of these is combined to derive a new N-dimensional vector. This represents the pSwitch's Perception of the suitability of the underlying vRM cooperative to accept new tasks. This Perception can be customised by choosing the specific manner in which the input N-dimensional vectors are combined. The resulting N-dimensional vector is passed to the pSwitch's pRouter.

3.4.2.3 Mechanism to Send Metrics from pRouter to Cell

A number of N-dimensional vectors will arrive at a pRouter (one from each pSwitch in the cooperative defined by that pRouter), and each of these is once again combined to derive an N-dimensional vector representing the local state of that pRouter. This state can be viewed as being the pRouters Perception of the suitability of the underlying pSwitch cooperative to accept new tasks. This perception can also be customised by choosing the specific manner in which the input N-dimensional vectors are combined. This N-dimensional vector is passed to the Cell.

3.4.2.4 Mechanism to Send Weights from Cell to pRouters

Weights sent from a level in the hierarchy to a lower level represent the desire of the transmitting level to evolve in a particular direction. Since the Cell is at the highest level in the hierarchy, the sending of weights to the pRouters is the first step in the process of Directed Evolution. There are many strategies that the Cell can employ to determine how these weights change from time to time in the CloudLightning system. In all cases, these weights are sent to each pRouter as an N-dimensional vector representing the desired/calculated change to the progression of the Directed Evolution.

3.4.2.5 Mechanism to Send Weights from pRouters to pSwitches

After receiving an updated N-dimensional vector from the Cell, a pRouter will transform it using a customizable function, which will dictate the rate at which the next level down in the hierarchy is expected to change. This transformed N-dimensional vector is passed to the underlying pSwitches.

3.4.2.6 Mechanism to Send Weights from pSwitch to vRMs

After receiving an updated N-dimensional vector from the pRouter, a pSwitch will transform it using a customizable function, which will dictate the rate at which the next level down in the hierarchy is expected to change. This transformed N-dimensional vector is passed to the underlying vRMs.

The same weights are propagated to every component in the same level (in the same pRouter). This ensures that the underlying level does not return metrics that cannot be meaningfully compared at that level. For example, if the weights associated with the calculations of power efficiency in two different servers of the same type are grossly different, one will appear to be more power efficient than the other even if both are equally power efficient.

Figure 3.4 depicts an example propagation of weights and metrics through the CL hierarchy in eight distinct time-steps. These vectors are propagated asynchronously from level to level. The metrics originate at the bottom level of the hierarchy, where they are derived from the application of CL-specific assessment functions applied to data gathered from the resource monitor. As they travel up through the hierarchy, they are aggregated to give successive perceptions of the underlying system at each successive component. The propagation of weights begins at the Cell and is modified as they are passed down through the hierarchy to reflect successive inflections of the Impetus coming from the Directed Evolution.

3.4.2.7 A Mechanism in the Cell to Modify Local Behaviour in an Effort to Respond to Impetus Provided by the Directed Evolution and Metrics Coming from Attached pRouters

Perception is a function such that:

$$\vec{P}_{Cell} = \varphi\left(\vec{m}_1, \vec{m}_2, \ldots, \vec{m}_r\right), \ \vec{m}_1 \in R^N, \ \vec{m}_2 \in R^N, \ \ldots, \ \vec{m}_r \in R^N \qquad (3.8)$$

Here, each $\vec{m}_i$ is a metric (an N-dimensional vector) coming from each of the $\mathbf{r}$ pRouters attached to the Cell.

Impetus $\vec{I}_{Cell} = \mu\left(T_i\right)$, where T_i is the task prescription under consideration.

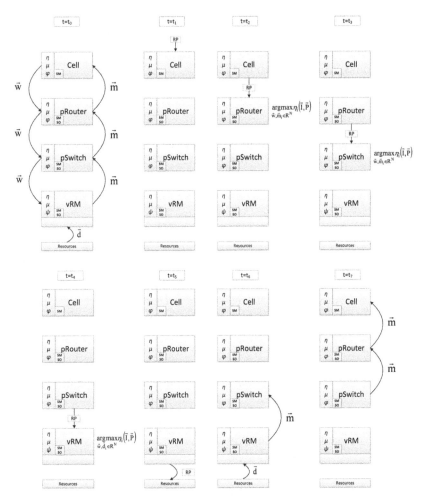

Fig. 3.4 An example propagation of weights and metrics through the CL hierarchy, with respect to a resource prescription

3.4.2.8 A Mechanism in a pRouter to Modify Local Behaviour
in an Effort to Respond to Impetus Transmitted by the Cell
and Metrics Coming from Attached pSwitches

Perception is a function such that:

$$\vec{P}_{pRouter} = \varphi\left(\vec{m}_1, \vec{m}_2, \ldots, \vec{m}_s\right), \ \vec{m}_1 \in R^N, \ \vec{m}_2 \in R^N, \ldots, \vec{m}_s \in R^N \quad (3.9)$$

Here, each $\vec{m}_i$ is a metric (an N-dimensional vector) coming from each of the **s** pSwitches attached to the pRouter.

Impetus is a function such that:

$$\vec{I}_{pRouter} = \mu\left(\vec{I}'_{pRouter}, \vec{I}_{Cell}\right), \ \vec{I}'_{pRouter} \in R^N, \ \vec{I}_{Cell} \in R^N \quad (3.10)$$

where $\vec{I}'_{pRouter}$ is the previous Impetus of the pRouter. Here $\vec{I}_{Cell}$ represents the weight coming from the Cell.

3.4.2.9 A Mechanism in a pSwitch to Modify Local Behaviour
in an Effort to Respond to Impetus Transmitted by its pRouter
and Metrics Coming from Attached vRMs

Perception is a function such that:

$$\vec{P}_{pSwitch} = \varphi\left(\vec{m}_1, \vec{m}_2, \ldots, \vec{m}_v\right), \ \vec{m}_1 \in R^N, \ \vec{m}_2 \in R^N, \ldots, \vec{m}_v \in R^N \quad (3.11)$$

Here, each $\vec{m}_i$ is a metric (an N-dimensional vector) coming from each of the **v** vRMs attached to the pSwitch.

Impetus is a function such that:

$$\vec{I}_{pSwitch} = \mu\left(\vec{I}'_{pSwitch}, \vec{I}_{pRouter}\right), \ \vec{I}'_{pSwitch} \in R^N, \ \vec{I}_{pRouter} \in R^N \quad (3.12)$$

where $\vec{I}'_{pSwitch}$ is the previous Impetus of the pSwitch. Here $\vec{I}_{pRouter}$ represents the weight coming from the pRouter.

3.4.2.10 A Mechanism in a vRM to Modify Local Behaviour in an Effort to Respond to Impetus Transmitted by its pSwitch and Metrics Coming from its vRack

Perception is a function such that:

$$\vec{P}_{vRM} = \vec{m} = \psi\left(\vec{d}\right),\ \vec{d} \in R^{M} \tag{3.13}$$

where $\vec{d}$ represents an M-dimensional Telemetry data obtained from the Telemetry service running on the physical resources belonging to the associated vRack.

Impetus is a function such that:

$$\vec{I}_{vRM} = \mu\left(\vec{I}'_{vRM}, \vec{I}_{pSwitch}\right),\ \vec{I}'_{vRM} \in R^{N},\ \vec{I}_{pSwitch} \in R^{N} \tag{3.14}$$

where $\vec{I}'_{vRM}$ is the previous Impetus of the vRM. Here $\vec{I}_{pSwitch}$ represents the weight coming from the pSwitch.

3.4.2.11 Sample Events that Trigger the Transmission of Metrics at each Level in the Hierarchy

Options:

- Periodically, at a rate suitable for that level in the hierarchy
- From the vRM to the pSwitch:
  - After the receipt of a task prescription
  - When resources are freed
  - As a result of a self-organisation activity
  - Periodically to reflect utilisation, power consumption, and other low-level metrics of interest

3.4.2.12 Sample Events that Trigger the Transmission of Weights at Each Level in the Hierarchy

Options:

- As a result of steering
- Periodically, at a rate appropriate for each level in the hierarchy

3.4.3   Self-Organisation Mechanisms

vRMs self-organise within the same pSwitch to optimally manage CL-Resources and to satisfy resource prescriptions, thus, maximising their SI and evolving towards the local goal state. Similarly, pSwitches can self-organise within the same pRouter to maximise their SI to identify those parts of the system that are evolving towards their local goals. In principle, pRouters of the same CL-Resource type can also self-organise; however, that level of re-organisation is not considered further here since the added advantages are thought to be minimal. One example of Self-organisation scenarios can be described as follows.

Within the vRMs

1.   A task comes into the pSwitch.
2.   The pSwitch sends the task to an attached vRM with the highest SI.
3.   The vRM checks to see if it has sufficient resources to execute the task.

  (a) If yes, no problem.
  (b) If no, the vRM initialises a self-organisation event within its cooperative.

4.   The vRMs send updated metrics with their pSwitch.

Within the pSwitches

1.   A task comes into the pRouter.
2.   The pRouter sends the task to an attached pSwitch with the highest SI.
3.   The pSwitch checks to see if there are sufficient resources to execute the task.

  (a) If yes, it passes the task to the vRM with the highest SI.
  (b) If no, the pSwitch initialises a self-organisation event within its co- operative.

4.   The pSwitch sends updated metrics to its pRouter.

Within the pRouter

1. A task comes into the Cell.
2. The Cell sends the task to an attached pRouter with the highest SI of the desired type.
3. The pRouter checks to see if there are sufficient resources to execute the task.

   (a) If yes, passes the task to the pSwitch with the highest SI.
   (b) If no, the pRouter initialises a self-organisation event within its co- operative.

4. The pRouter sends updated metrics to the Cell.

Sample events that trigger re-organisation at each level in the hierarchy

- When weights are updated.
- As a result of an autonomous, periodic, housekeeping action designed to maximise the SI of the initiating component.
- After the arrival of a resource prescription that cannot be satisfied without re-organisation.

When all else fails: sample resource prescription rejection strategies

- Outright reject.
- Return prescription to the previous level and possibly trigger a re-organisation there.
- Recycle the task prescription into the system at the Cell level and record its recycle iterations until an upper limit is reached. If this limit is reached, reject.

3.5   CLOUDLIGHTNING SOSM STRATEGIES

3.5.1   Self-Management Strategies

In the CloudLightning SOSM framework, each component is autonomous, which allows the component using different self-management strategies accordingly to achieve its local goal state.

Some self-management strategies may include:

- Static weights and dynamic weights (only for Cell Manager)
- Average aggregation (suitable for pRouters, pSwitches, and vRMs)
- Modifying weights for smoothing changes towards local goal state (suitable for pRouters, pSwitches, and vRMs)
- Bin-packing for energy efficiency (only for vRMs)
- Functions for management efficiency (only for vRMs)
- Isotropy preservation for task process parallelism (only for vRMs)

3.5.1.1 An Example Self-Management Scenario
Here, an example of examining the effect of different choices of management cost functions is presented. Four different functions are selected for inspection, characterising different types of evolution, which are described by the equations that follow.

(a)   Small vRacks

$$1 - \int_{0}^{\frac{2N_{total}}{N_{total}-2}} e^{-t^2} dt \tag{3.15}$$

Equation 3.15 favours small capacity vRacks enabling them to evolve; while when a vRack has large capacity, the output of the management cost function approaches zero resulting in a reduced SI. Thus, large vRacks are not capable of undertaking more requests, and they have to transfer their servers to other smaller vRacks in order to slowly achieve the ideal size.

(b)   Large vRacks

$$1 - \int_{0}^{\frac{2\left(2\hat{N}_{total}-N_{total}\right)}{\hat{N}_{total}-2}} e^{-t^2} dt \tag{3.16}$$

Equation 3.16 favours large capacity vRacks; when a vRack has small capacity, the output of the management cost function approaches zero resulting in a reduced SI. Thus, small vRacks are not capable of undertaking more requests, and they have to transfer their servers to other larger vRacks merging with them.

(c) Medium vRacks

$$e^{-\frac{\left(-4+4\frac{N_{total}}{\hat{N}_{total}}\right)^2}{2}} \tag{3.17}$$

Equation 3.17 favours medium capacity vRacks; when a vRack has very small or very large capacity, the output of the management cost function approaches zero resulting in a reduced SI. Thus, very small and very large vRacks are not capable of undertaking more requests, and they have to transfer their servers or merge with other vRacks.

(d) Extreme vRacks

$$1 - e^{-\frac{\left(-4+4\frac{N_{total}}{\hat{N}_{total}}\right)^2}{2}} \tag{3.18}$$

Equation 3.18 favours very small capacity or very large capacity vRacks; when a vRack has medium capacity, the output of the management cost function approaches zero resulting in a reduced SI. Thus, medium capacity vRacks are not capable of undertaking more requests, and they have to transfer their servers or merge with other smaller or larger vRacks.

Overall, the optimal number of servers per vRack is given by $\hat{N}_{total} = \frac{1}{N_v}\sum_{i=1}^{N_v}(N_{total})_i$. This number is dynamic and is changing with the creation/destruction of vRacks or with the merging/splitting of vRacks. The management cost functions can be depicted schematically by (a), (b), (c), and (d) in Fig. 3.5.

However, the choice of management cost function significantly affects the evolution as well as other parameters and metrics of the systems such as utilisation and number of rejected resource prescriptions.

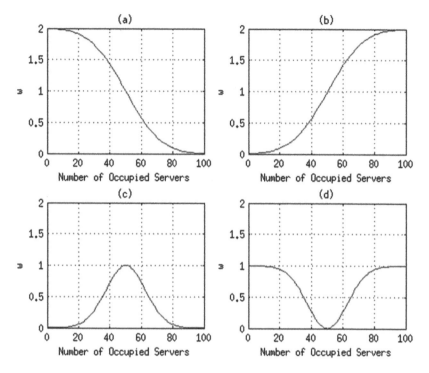

Fig. 3.5   Different types of management cost functions

3.5.2   Self-Organisation Strategies

The self-organising components in the system include vRMs and pSwitches. vRMs self-organise within the same pSwitch to optimally manage CL-Resources and to satisfy resource prescriptions, thus maximising their SI and evolving towards the local goal state. Similarly, pSwitches can self-organise within the same pRouter to maximise their SI to identify those parts of the system that are evolving towards their local goals. In principle, pRouters of the same CL-Resource type can also self-organise; however, that level of re-organisation is not considered further in this book since the added advantages are thought to be minimal.

Some self-organisation strategies may include:

- *Dominate*: the component with the greater SI has precedence and can demand another component of the same type, but with a lower SI, to transfer some resources.
- *Win-Win*: components may cooperate to exchange resources to maximise the SI of each.
- *Least Disruptive*: minimise disruption with respect to management and administration.
- *Balanced*: maximise load-balancing among each cooperating component.
- *Best Fit*: minimise server fragmentation and/or minimise network latency (this strategy may come from some vRM-specific objectives).
- Any meaningful combination of the above.

3.5.2.1 An Example Self-Organisation Scenario

An example of a Least Disruptive algorithm that can be used by vRMs for self-organisation is presented. This algorithm can be used by vRMs to exchange resources to minimise their management cost. This algorithm has two steps: the first function endeavours each vRM to minimise the number of administrative actions, and the second function is taking virtualisation and fragmentation into account, which can be used to avoid the creation of very large vRMs for management efficiency purpose. This two-stage self-organising scheme can be described by the algorithmic procedure given by the following algorithm.

Algorithm 1

Let ρ be the minimum number of vRacks allowed per pSwitch

Let j be the index of the vRack with maximum Suitability Index

Let rp be a resource prescription arriving to vRM_j

Let p_j be the set of free resources belonging to vRM_j

function MINADMINCOSTS(rp)

    $a = \emptyset$

    $t = \emptyset$

  if $p_j < rp$ **then**

      $required = rp\text{-}|p_j|$

      for $i \leftarrow 1$ to N_v with $i \neq j$ **do**

        send request to acquire free resources from vRM_i

        receive p_i from vRM_i

        $a = a \cup \{i\}$

        $t = t \cup p_i$

        if $required \leq 0$ **then**

          remove exceeding resources from t

          $required = 0$

          break

      send request to vRMs in a to acquire resources in t

      receive resource handlers from vRMs in a

      if $|p_j| \geq \frac{rp}{2}$ **then**

        return *resource handlers to Gateway Service*

      else

        create new vRM_k with resources $p_i \cup t$

        return *resource handlers to Gateway Service*

function TWOSTAGESO(rp)

  if MINADMINCOSTS(rp) does not return *resource handlers* **then**

    if $|p_j| \leq \widehat{N}_u$ and $N_u \geq \rho$ **then**

      for $i \leftarrow 1$ to N_u with $i \neq j$ **do**

        Probe ith vRM *for resources, so that $p_j \cup p_i$ can service rp*

        if $p_j \cup p_i$ *can service rp* **then**

          Merge vRM_i with vRM_j

          return *resource handler from resulting vRM to Gateway Service*

            rejection to Gateway Service

    else

      return *resource handlers obtained from* MINADMINCOSTS(rp) *to Gateway Service*

Figure 3.6 presents the increased system utilisation and requests reject rate of this two-stage self-organisation algorithm merging with the minimum free resources. However, because the system accommodates larger tasks through merging, the smaller tasks arriving at the system are continuously rejected due to lack of resources.

In the case of merging with the vRack with maximum free resources, the utilisation of the system, depicted in Fig. 3.7a, is slightly increased but oscillates around 80%. As a consequence, the percentage of rejected requests increases, since the system is accommodating an increased number of larger requests, as schematically represented in Fig. 3.7b.

Overall, this two-stage self-organisation strategy has been employed for enhancing utilisation and reducing fragmentation with virtualisation in mind.

3.6 CONCLUSION

The SOSM framework described in this chapter provides a general and scalable mechanism for hosting and executing SOSM strategies that, in principle, could be associated with any hierarchical architecture.

The key elements of the self-management and self-organisation framework include the process of Directed Evolution; an Impetus that drives the evolutionary process at all levels in the hierarchy; a Perception, associated with each component, indicating the effectiveness of the system underlying that component; and an SI, associated with each component, that determines how close that component is to achieving its goal state. Specifying an objective global goal state may be based on business decisions and/or technology constraints, however, to optimise the CloudLightning system in its entirety; it is suggested that the goal states for components of the system should be chosen to maximise their respective SIs.

This approach introduces a great deal of flexibility into the evolution of a system by allowing it to achieve stasis while attempting to balance local constraints with the external Impetus derived from the directed evolutionary process. Over time, the system as a whole evolves to optimise typical service usage, to achieve the dynamic equilibrium. The local constraints are most evident at the vRM level where they are embodied in assessment functions capturing the essential characteristics of the underlying resources.

The framework endows the system being specified with the flexibility to extend the resource fabric in a seamless fashion. This elegantly addresses the CloudLightning objective of readily supporting heterogeneous hardware now and into the future.

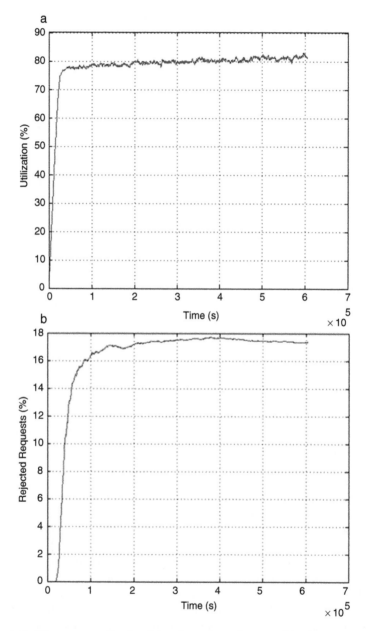

Fig. 3.6 The system utilisation (**a**) and requests reject rate (**b**) of two-stage self-organisation algorithm merging with the minimum free resources ($\rho = 3$)

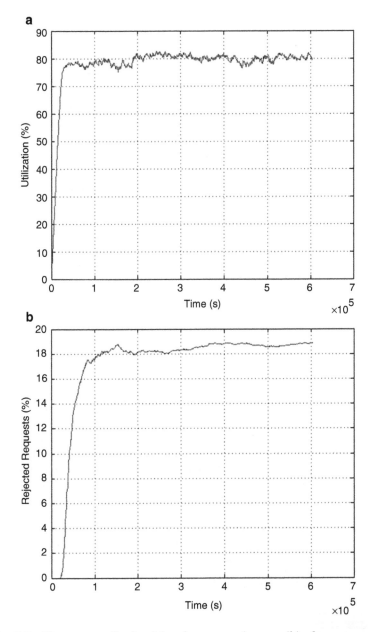

Fig. 3.7 The system utilisation (**a**) and requests reject rate (**b**) of two-stage self-organisation algorithm merging with the maximum free resources ($\rho = 3$)

3.7   Chapter 3 Related CloudLightning Readings

1. Drăgan, I., Fortiş, T. F., Iuhasz, G., Neagul, M., & Petcu, D. (2017). Applying self-* principles in heterogeneous cloud environments. *Cloud Computing*, 255–274. Springer International Publishing.
2. Filelis-Papadopoulos, C., Xiong, H., Spataru, A., Castane, G., Dong, D., Gravvanis, G., et al. (2017, July). A generic framework supporting self-organisation and self-management in hierarchical systems. In *The 16th International Symposium on Parallel and Distributed Computing (ISPDC 2017)*. Innsbruck, Austria.
3. Petcu, D. (2015). On autonomic HPC Clouds. In *Proceedings of the Second International Workshop on Sustainable Ultrascale Computing Systems (NESUS 2015)* (pp. 29–40).
4. Stack, P., Xiong, H., Mersel, D., Makhloufi, M., Terpend, G., & Dong, D. (2017). Self-healing in a decentralised Cloud management system. In *Proceedings of the 1st International Workshop on Next generation of Cloud Architectures*, Vol. 3. ACM.

CHAPTER 4

Application Blueprints and Service Description

Ioan Dragan, Teodor-Florin Fortiş, Marian Neagul, Dana Petcu, Teodora Selea, and Adrian Spataru

Abstract In the context of creating a self-organising and self-managing cloud infrastructure we propose a set of extensions to the existing Service Description Languages (SDLs) and Application Blueprints in order to establish a common ground for the various CloudLightning components. By implementing this SDL and all the missing links one can assure that the CloudLightning system works in such a way that users can easily interact with it. In this chapter we present in detail the design decisions that were made during the development of various components alongside with their formal description.

I. Dragan (✉)
Victor Babeş University of Medicine and Pharmacy, Timişoara, Romania

Institute e-Austria Timisoara, Timişoara, Romania
e-mail: idragan@ieat.ro

T.-F. Fortiş • M. Neagul • D. Petcu • T. Selea • A. Spataru
Institute e-Austria Timisoara, Timişoara, Romania

West University of Timişoara, Timişoara, Romania
e-mail: florin.fortis@e-uvt.ro; marian.neagul@e-uvt.ro; Dana.Petcu@e-uvt.ro; adrian.spataru@e-uvt.ro

T. Lynn et al. (eds.), *Heterogeneity, High Performance Computing, Self-Organization and the Cloud*, Palgrave Studies in Digital Business & Enabling Technologies,
https://doi.org/10.1007/978-3-319-76038-4_4

Keywords Service Description Language • CL Blueprints • CL Gateway Service • Lifecycle and resource management

4.1   INTRODUCTION

To deliver the quality of service (QoS) expected by end users on a distributed multi-tenant infrastructure requires careful management of computing resources. This is particularly the case where there is a rapid growth in usage such as cloud computing. Cloud service providers (CSPs) are faced with a myriad of challenges in meeting the needs of a large and diverse range of end users including, but not limited to, service transparency, automated service provisioning, efficiently managing workload segmentation and portability, and managing virtual services instances at one level, while optimising the utilisation of all resources at a different level (Sun et al. 2012). The issues can be resolved through specialised and precise cloud service specification models, Service Description Languages (SDLs), describing cloud services, their deployment specifications, and the required resources to run these cloud services. The majority of the existing SDLs and associated frameworks implement tools, Application Programming Interfaces (APIs), and strategies for managing the lifecycle of cloud applications and/or resources, and they are usually provided as a self-service interface to Enterprise Application Operators (EAOs). This self-service approach allows an EAO to have full control over the management of applications as well as the underlying resources such as virtual machines (VMs) and containers. It subsequently narrows down the opportunities for CSPs to improve resource utilisation and potentially the quality of services.

The CloudLightning architecture endeavours to create a service-oriented architecture for the evolving heterogeneous cloud. In this respect, it is imperative to maintain a separation between application lifecycle management and resource management. This separation of concerns implements a "what-how" approach where the user concentrates on "what" needs to be done, while the CSP concentrates on "how" it should be done. With such an approach, it will be possible to implement continuous improvements, in terms of resource utilisation and service delivery, at the resource level. From this perspective, SDLs facilitate both (a) application lifecycle management by the user and (b) resource management by the CSP. As such, they ensure a proper separation of concerns between stakeholders, a core design principle of CloudLightning introduced in Chap. 1. Particular service offerings are captured in blueprints to assist end users to discover and select from an increasing catalogue of services and determine an optimal, and potentially heterogeneous, set of resources to implement them. The remainder of this chapter is organised as follows. The next section provides an overview of two representative application lifecycle frameworks and one representative resource management framework. This is followed by an overview of the specific stakeholders whose concerns are of interest to CloudLightning. The CloudLightning approach to separation of concerns is then described followed by the Gateway Service and its functionalities. Formal definition of the CloudLightning Service Description Language (CL-SDL) is provided in Sect. 4.4 followed by an exemplar implementation. This chapter concludes with a summary and future work on the components and concepts presented in the chapter.

4.2   REPRESENTATIVE APPLICATION LIFECYCLE AND RESOURCE MANAGEMENT FRAMEWORKS

In order to identify concerns about the classical, vertical management approach to cloud computing application lifecycle and resource management, three representative frameworks are used for illustrative purposes: OpenStack Solum, Apache Brooklyn, and OpenStack Heat.

The cloud application lifecycle management architecture is represented in Fig. 4.1, using OpenStack Solum and Apache Brooklyn frameworks for Platform as a Service (PaaS) cloud, and resource lifecycle management using OpenStack Heat mainly for Infrastructure as a Service (IaaS) cloud.

Project Solum and Apache Brooklyn allow the user to deploy a cloud application or a group of cloud applications previously described in a blueprint, using an SDL. The main purpose of such an SDL is to provide a way of expressing the management processes for cloud applications. Depending on the actual implementations, this may include providing the ability for describing the characteristics of the application components, deployments scripting, dependencies, locations, logging, policies, and so on.

In the case of OpenStack Solum, the engine takes a blueprint as an input and converts it to a Heat Orchestration Template (HOT) that can be understood by the application and resource management engine (OpenStack Heat). The Heat engine, thereafter, calls the corresponding service APIs that are offered by the cloud infrastructure framework such as OpenStack.

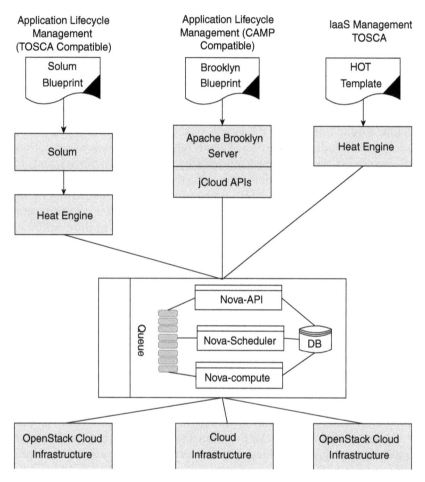

Fig. 4.1 Lifecycle management for OpenStack Solum, Apace Brooklyn, and OpenStack Heat

In contrast, Apache Brooklyn converts a blueprint into a series of API calls (specifically, jCloud APIs) that can be used to directly contact the underlying cloud infrastructure. For example, these calls may reach the cloud infrastructure with a request for creating a VM in OpenStack; the OpenStack Nova API service will capture the request and send it to nova-scheduler, which, in turn, decides on the physical server on which the VM should be started on. This approach is based on a request-response pattern, providing a simple, robust, and efficient implementation. However, as each request is processed independently, when blueprints are specifying, for example, placement constraints based on vicinity of resources, such a constraint is hard to be captured and fully implemented by APIs with a vertical approach.

4.3   CloudLightning Stakeholders and Associated Concerns

Separation of concerns requires the identification of stakeholders and their associated concerns. For illustrative purposes, three distinct entities are identified—end users, Enterprise Application Operators and Developers (EAO/EAD), and IaaS resource providers (CSPs) each with differing concerns. The end user is the consumer of an application and/or service. As such, their concerns are primarily related to cloud application continuity, availability, performance, security, and business logic correctness. The EAO/EAD has traditional enterprise concerns, for example, cloud application configuration management, performance, load balancing, security, availability, and the deployment environment. As discussed in Chap. 1, the CSP's business model is driven by cost effectiveness and scalability while at the same time delivering the contracted service level. As such, their concerns are primarily related to optimisation including resource availability, operating costs (including power consumption), resource provisioning, resource organisation, and partitioning (if applicable).

Under separation of concerns, each entity manages their own concerns, to the extent that they can. Notwithstanding this, some concerns exist across the entities. For example, in order to realise high availability, an EAO may need to configure a load-balancer, while at the same time a CSP must implement a host-affinity policy.

4.4   The CloudLightning Approach Based on Separation of Concerns

4.4.1   CloudLightning Requirements

As discussed, the CloudLightning service delivery model depicted in Fig. 4.2 is a blueprint-based one. In contrast to existing frameworks, this service delivery model provides facilities for blueprint developers to specify

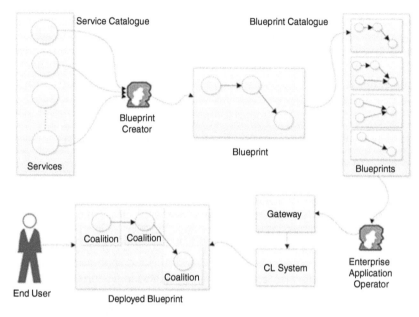

Fig. 4.2   CloudLightning service delivery model

comprehensive constraints and quality of service parameters for services and/or resources in the scope of a blueprint, by means of a specific SDL (the CL-SDL). Based on the specified constraints and parameters, it is then possible to provide an initial optimal deployment of the resources, a capability which has not been accomplished by previous solutions: for example, by placing resources (such as VMs) on the adjacent physical servers to minimise communication delay or allocating containers that have Graphical Processing Units (GPUs) or Xeon Phis attached to them to balance between performance and cost.

More importantly, in order to separate the concerns of cloud application lifecycle management and the resource lifecycle management, a CloudLightning-specific blueprint (CL-Blueprint) must be decomposed into two separate and interrelated blueprints, the first one for resource management (offering the Resource Template) and the other one for application/workflow management (defining framework-specific templates). This process is shown in Fig. 4.3. It also implies that the

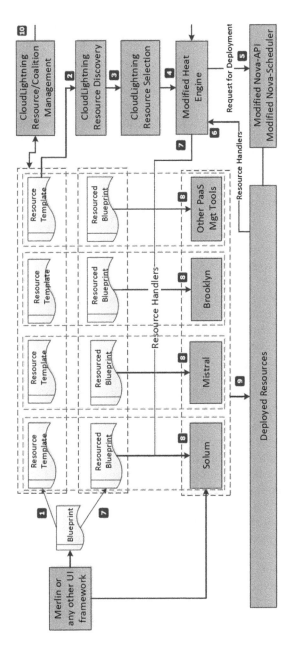

Fig. 4.3 Architecture for CloudLightning service delivery

CL-SDL shall be developed in such a way that a CL-Blueprint described in the CL-SDL can be transformed to framework-specific blueprints without losing generality.

A CL-Blueprint deployment starts from sending the raw Resource Template to a Resource Discovery component and a Resource Selection component, which are the two main components of a complementary system (in this situation, the CloudLightning Self-Organising and Self-Management [SOSM] framework), for optimal resource identification in the scope of a blueprint, as indicated in Fig. 4.3. Once the optimal resource identification process has finished, the initially received Resource Template must be reconstructed in order to embed the received resource optimisation information and consequently send it to the resource lifecycle management engine, which will carry out the actual resource deployment on the infrastructure it manages.

In addition, some of the optimisation information (e.g., on which physical server should this VM be allocated) must be embedded into resource requests (API calls), and this special information must be captured by the lower infrastructure management components.

The returns from the deployment process are the resource handlers (e.g., a resource handler can be a login account with username, access key, and Internet Protocol address to a VM, a container, a bare metal machine with pre-installed operating system, or an existing High Performance Computing [HPC] cluster). These resource handlers will then be returned to the Gateway Service, which will reformulate the original workflow/application blueprint along with the resource handlers.

The newly formulated workflow/application blueprint will then be submitted to the corresponding workflow/application lifecycle management framework to carry out the deployment of the cloud applications on these pre-provisioned resources. This process is shown in Fig. 4.3. To this end, a CL-Blueprint deployment process is complete.

Notice that this service delivery model is much more sophisticated when compared to the current self-service model using a vertical management approach, as the cloud application management and the resource management operate independently. Moreover, the cloud application management layer constantly needs to exchange information with resource management layers in certain circumstances (e.g., when ending the lifetime of a CL-Blueprint, a notification needs to be sent to the resource management layer so that the underlying resources can be reused or decommissioned).

In order to align with the design of the bespoke service delivery model, and implement the separation of concerns, the specific SDL shall be developed with following capabilities:

1. To describe characteristics of a cloud application
2. To describe cloud application execution environment and dependencies
3. To specify cloud application deployment processes
4. To specify resource type and resource requirements
5. To express constraints between blueprint service elements
6. To express quality of service parameters for each individual blueprint service element
7. To accommodate extensions for supporting specific/non-traditional cloud applications such as HPC applications
8. To fulfil above requirements without losing generality

4.4.2   Separation of Concerns

During the lifetime of the CL-Blueprint, the EADs/EAOs are responsible for managing the cloud applications through specific frameworks, such as Apache Brooklyn and OpenStack Solum, while the CloudLightning SOSM system manages the underlying resources. A series of advantages of this approach may be then highlighted:

1. continuous improvement on quality of CL-Blueprint services
2. improving service delivery and user experience by reusing resources that have already been provisioned
3. resource optimisations and energy efficiency optimisation
4. flexible and extensible when integrating other management system such as the OpenStack Mistral (Openstack.org 2017) workflow management system

In CloudLightning, the functional components that realise the concept of the "separation of concerns" are shown in Fig. 4.4 with the following description.

4.4.2.1   Application Lifecycle Management

- *Abstract Blueprint*: used to represent specific application requirements, constraints, and metrics defined by users, and describe

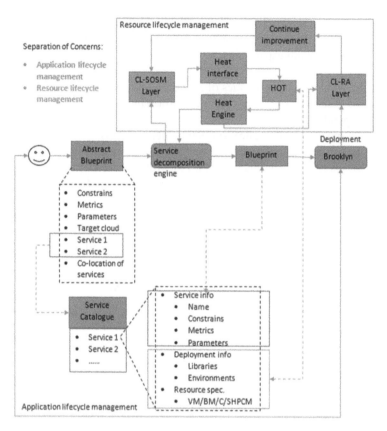

Fig. 4.4   CloudLightning implementation of the "separation of concerns"

the concrete and abstract services (referenced only by identification) alongside with the collocation of the services.

- *Blueprint*: represents a fully qualified Cloud Application Management for Platforms (CAMP) (Organization for the Advancement of Structured Information Standards [OASIS] CAMP TC, 2014) Document containing references to real resource types, resource locations, and deployment mechanisms, which are fully understood and handled by a CAMP-compliant implementation.
- *Service Catalogue*: it is a persistent collection of versioned services, each of which includes service information, deployment information, and CL-Resource specification.

- *Service Decomposition Engine (SDE)*: handles the transformation of Abstract Blueprints to concrete Blueprints according to provided requirements.
- *Brooklyn*: used for deploying and managing the applications via Blueprints.

4.4.2.2 Resource Lifecycle Management

- *CL-SOSM Layer*: CloudLightning SOSM Layer aims to identify and create/allocate the optimal CL-Resource for applications using principles of SOSM.
- *CL-RA Layer*: CloudLightning Resource Abstraction Layer is used for abstracting the CL-Resources in different ways (such as Bare Metal, Virtualisation, Containerisation, and Direct Access) from various hardware types (such as Central Processing Unit [CPU], GPU, Data Flow Engine, and Many Integrated Core [MIC]).
- *Heat Orchestration Template (HOT)*: describes the infrastructure resource (such as servers, networks, routers, floating IPs, and volume) for a cloud application, as well as the relationships between resources.
- *Heat Interface*: automatically generates HOTs in terms of the results from SOSM Layer or dynamically modifies HOTs based on the results from the Continued Improvement component.
- *Heat Engine*: manages the whole lifecycle of the provisioning process.
- *Continued Improvement*: this management component together with Heat and telemetry does the continued improvement for the deployed blueprint during the lifetime.

4.5   THE CLOUDLIGHTNING GATEWAY ARCHITECTURE

Integration of the use cases provided in CloudLightning with the Gateway Service will be done by following the CL-SDL (Xiong et al. 2016). The proposed CL-SDL specification is built on top of the OASIS CAMP specification and introduces new concepts suitable for expressing the requirements of HPC applications.

The syntax of the CL-SDL is based on the Brooklyn blueprint YAML (Yet Another Markup Language) and is used to describe the Resource Template and the Resourced Blueprint. Both of these offer support for CloudLightning Blueprint lifecycle management.

The Blueprint is used to represent specific application requirements, constraints, and metrics defined by either the EAD or the EAO, and describe services by name and their relationships. As depicted in Fig. 4.5, service definitions are predefined by EADs in special catalogues that follow the Cloud Service Archive (CSAR) specifications (Breiter et al. 2012), a subset of rules defined by the Topology and Orchestration Specification for Cloud Applications (TOSCA) standard (OASIS Open 2013).

The Resourced Blueprint is obtained from the SDE. This operation effectively invokes the underlying CL-SOSM subsystem that is responsible for resource management, for available resources and resource definitions. The resulting Resourced Blueprint is completely supported by a CAMP-compliant CAMP Provider (Carlson et al. 2012).[1]

In the CL-Blueprint all references to CloudLightning-defined artefacts are removed, except for specific CloudLightning handles (opaque to the CAMP Provider). These handles are used for the creation of a session between the resource scheduling (self-organisation) layer and the deployed resources. This CL-Blueprint represents a fully qualified CAMP Document containing reference to real resource types, resource locations, and deployment mechanisms, which are fully understood and handled by a CAMP-compliant implementation.

4.5.1   Gateway Service Architecture

The CloudLightning Gateway Service builds upon the capabilities of the Apache Brooklyn solution, providing "service decomposition" capabilities. The Gateway Service completely reuses the rest of the features provided by Apache Brooklyn, facilitating the reuse of existing Blueprints and integration. Of particular interest is the integration with various Configuration Management Systems like Puppet, Chef, or Ansible (Fig. 4.6).

The Gateway Service has several roles, as follows:

1. Receive/create abstract[2] Blueprint definitions from EAO.
2. Decompose the received Abstract Blueprint into individual services. For each of the services check if it is a fully qualified service or has to be further processed. This operation is further discussed in Sect. 4.5.2 (Service Decomposition).
3. Once the Blueprint is fully qualified (it does not contain any abstract service definitions), the Gateway Service triggers the services deployment and further execution.

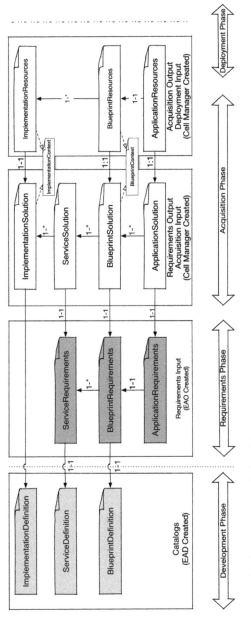

Fig. 4.5 API Message relationships

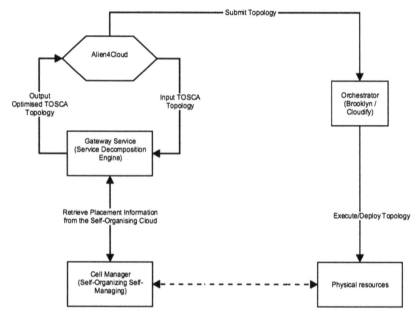

Fig. 4.6   Gateway Service overall architecture

The Gateway Service exposes a series of APIs usable by consumers (EAOs and EADs) for controlling the application lifecycle.

4.5.2   Service Decomposition

The operation of Service Decomposition is implemented by the SDE and represents one of the core CloudLightning contributions in the Gateway Service. The SDE is responsible for the interaction with the SOSM subsystem. The overall operation of the SDE can be summarised as follows:

1. For each service, check if it can be instantiated directly (there exists a single implementation of the service, and that implementation is well known to the Gateway Service) or that it is an abstract service (a service interface that could be implemented by several implementations).
2. If the service is an abstract service the SDE contacts the backend SOSM system for selecting the proper implementations for the service.

3. In order to facilitate the selection of the proper implementation, the SDE transmits the user-provided requirements (in the form of ClassAd [Solomon 2003] definitions). These requirements are used by the SOSM subsystem for properly selecting the right implementations.

4. The selection of concrete implementations results in modifying the original Blueprint, by replacing the abstract definition with the resourced one (eventually after a user interaction for validating the right solution) and submitting the Blueprint to the next stage.

4.5.3   Interaction with the SOSM System

After the successful query of available implementations for each abstract service definition, the SDE component constructs a Resource Template containing information about the specific requirements of each implementation. An example of such Resource Template is given in Listing 4.1

Consider a Blueprint containing a single service in order to maintain better readability of the listing. Such a document contains a **blueprint ID** that is unique for each request, a **timestamp** representing the request time, a **cost** limit for the entire Blueprint, and the **callback endpoint** used by the SOSM system to communicate back results of the optimisation steps.

The sample service has two implementation options between which the SOSM will choose depending on their constraints and the overall cost of the blueprint. The first one refers to the need for a single VM with a single core (expressed by a computation range between 1 and 1), 1000 MB of memory, 50 GB of storage, bandwidth between 100 Mbps and 1 Gbps, and no accelerators.

The second implementation is of type **MIC-CONTAINER**, requiring the CellManager to find or create a container, which has access to an **MIC** accelerator. This service requires one container with one CPU core, memory between 100 and 1000 MB, storage between 10 and 50 GB, the same bandwidth as the other implementation, and one MIC accelerator.

4.5.3.1   Resource Discovery
The Gateway Service and the SOSM system exchange information for two operations: *resource discovery* and *resource release*.

• *Resource discovery* is the operation by which the SOSM system chooses the most suitable service implementation and the resources on which to deploy it, according to user constraints and system state.

```
    "blueprintId": "{bpId}",
 2  "timestamp": 1929292,
    "cost": 0.0,
 4  "callbackEndpoint": "http://10.0.0.1/sde/rest/blueprints/{bpId}",
    "serviceElements": [
 6          {
                    "serviceElementId": "service-elem-1",
 8                  "implementations": [
                            {
10                              "implementationType": "CPU-VM",
                                "requiredResourceUnit": 1,
12                              "computationRange": [1, 1],
                                "memoryRange": [1000, 1000],
14                              "storageRange": [50, 50],
                                "bandwidthRange": [100, 1000],
16                              "acceleratorRange": [0, 0]
                            },

18
                            {
20                              "implementationType": "MIC-CONTAINER",
                                "requiredResourceUnit": 1,
22                              "computationRange": [1, 1],
                                "memoryRange": [100, 1000],
24                              "storageRange": [10, 50],
                                "bandwidthRange": [100, 1000],
26                              "acceleratorRange": [1, 1]
                            }
28                  ]
            },
30          ...
            ]
32  }
```

Listing 4.1   Resource template

- *Resource release* is the operation by which the SOSM system is informed that the services have been terminated, so the underlying resources may be reallocated.

The aforementioned operations are modelled by Hypertext Transfer Protocol (HTTP) Representational State Transfer (REST) methods, both the *Cell Manager* and the SDE acting as REST servers.

Figure 4.7 describes the protocol for resource discovery and a POST request with the body containing a ResourceTemplate of the structure, as illustrated in Listing 4.1. If the *Cell Manager* encounters any problems during the parsing of the body, the status code of the response will be **409 Conflict**. Otherwise, the status code will be **201 Created** and the resource

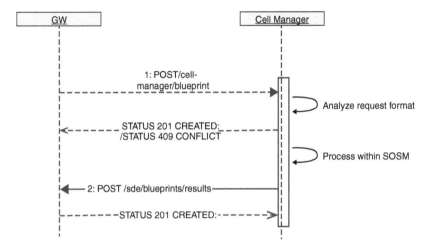

Fig. 4.7   Resource discovery sequence diagram

discovery process will start. The *Cell Manager* is in charge of informing the SDE when the result is ready.

When resources have been identified for all services, the *Cell Manager* will use a POST request with the body containing the information about the placement and implementation of each service, referred as a *Resourced Template*. This will trigger the SDE to instantiate each abstract service and update the Blueprint with concrete services and resource access information. An example result is shown in Listing 4.2. The chosen implementation is **CPU-VM**, and the resource type is **OPENSTACK ACCOUNT**, meaning that the SOSM is managing an OpenStack cluster as a resource. In this case, access information consists of credentials for accessing the OpenStack Nova API in order to create the VM.

4.5.3.2   Resource Release
The protocol for releasing the resources associated to a Blueprint is depicted in Fig. 4.8. A **DELETE** request is made to the *Cell Manager* at a path referencing the Blueprint ID. In case of successful resource release, the response will have the status **204 No Content**. Otherwise, the response will have status **400 Bad Request** and the body should provide useful information that will be propagated to the user interface (UI).

```
  {
2 "blueprintId": "{bpId}",
  "timestamp": 1929392,
4 "status": "SUCCESSFUL",
  "resourcedServiceElements": [
6        {
               "serviceElementId": "service-elem-1",
8              "implementationType": "CPU-VM",
               "creatorId": "vrm-1",
10             "status": "COMPLETED",
               "resourceType": "OPENSTACK_ACCOUNT",
12             "resources": [
               {
14             "resourceCreationId": "1234-5567-82929",
               "resourceDescriptor": "{\"platform\": \"OPENSTACK\",
16             \"domain\": \"SOSM\", \"project\": \"CL-SOSM\",
               \"username\": \"cl-admin\", \"password\": \"s3cret\",
18             \"authEndpoint\": \"http://10.0.2.19:5000/v3.0\"}"
               }
20             ]
        },
22
  ]
24 }
```

Listing 4.2   Resourced template

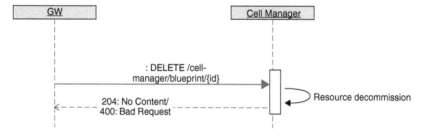

Fig. 4.8   Resource release sequence diagram

4.6   The CloudLightning Blueprint Extensions

Below is a summary of the technologies upon which the CloudLightning Blueprints were developed.

4.6.1   CloudLightning Brooklyn Extensions

As part of CloudLightning project, Apache Brooklyn was adopted and extended as the underlying platform for achieving the project's ultimate goal of both supporting HPC applications and adoption of modern cloud technologies, thus creating a bridge between the HPC and Cloud end user communities.

The decision to use the Apache Brooklyn framework is motivated by the design decisions established in the conceptualisation of the CloudLightning architecture (Morrison et al. 2016), the CloudLightning protocol specification and APIs (Neagul et al. 2016), and the Gateway Service (Dragan et al. 2017).

The main advantages of using Apache Brooklyn include:

1. It provides the building blocks needed for developing the necessary functionality expected from the Gateway Service.
2. It offers support for "automatic blueprints" based on OASIS CAMP, an extensible specification that can serve as the core specification for the CloudLightning Blueprints.
3. The Apache Project plans to support TOSCA in the near future.[3] This could potentially allow further developments in the CloudLightning SDL, supporting the TOSCA standard (OASIS Open 2013).
4. The harnessing of existing Apache Blueprints, providing HPC vendors more choices without requiring more development effort.

The purpose of this section is to discuss how the adoption of the Brooklyn Blueprints, particularly the expected additions to the Blueprint YAML, is envisioned in CloudLightning. As previously noted, two different kinds of blueprints are identified for use in CloudLightning: Abstract Blueprints and Concrete Blueprints (referred further as "blueprints"). Both types of Blueprints are built on top of Apache Brooklyn blueprints.

The translation between the Abstract Blueprint and Runnable Blueprints is performed by means of a specialised component residing inside the Gateway Service, component named "Service Decomposition Engine." The decomposition engine is responsible for interacting with the SOSM infrastructure (Fig. 4.9).

Each of the two types of Blueprints is discussed in the following sections, outlining the changes to the vanilla (plain) Brooklyn Blueprints. Note that the proposed extensions are subject to change as other parts of the CloudLightning Project evolve and might also be influenced by outside changes in the Apache Brooklyn project, as, for example, the addition of new functionality or deprecation of a current one.

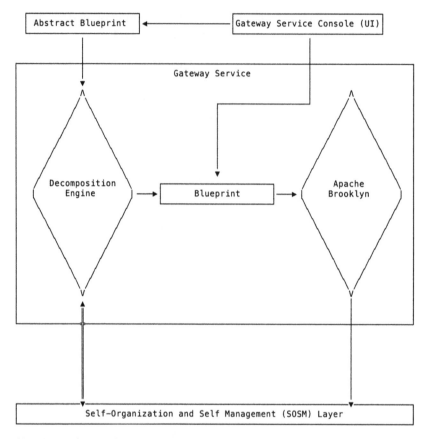

Fig. 4.9   CloudLightning Blueprint decomposition process

4.6.2   *CloudLightning Abstract Blueprint*

The Abstract Blueprint is represented by an extended version of the Apache Brooklyn Blueprint, containing attributes holding CloudLightning-specific entries, as described in Listing 4.3.

In this example, the Abstract Blueprint requires the deployment of a Java web application and a computing resource providing raytracing capabilities. Of interest in this case is the abstract computing service identified by the name "RaytracingApplicationId": the service cannot be directly handled by the Apache Brooklyn framework as it does not

```
   id:  jetty-node-with-raytracing-compute
 2 name:  "Jetty Application With Raytracing Computing Resource"
   origin:  http://cloudlightning.io/
 4 locations:
   - cloudlightning-openstack
 6 services:
   - type:  cloudlightning.entity.meta.RaytracingApp
 8 name:  RaytracingApplicationId
   location:  cloudlightning-openstack
10 cloudlightning.config:
   service-requirements:
12 - type:  classad
   requirement:  'Arch=="Intel" && CoProcesor=="IntelPhi"'
14 rank:  'TARGET.Mips'
   - type:  brooklyn.entity.webapp.ControlledDynamicWebAppCluster
16 name:  webApp
   location:  cloudlightning-openstack
18 cloudlightning.config:
   service-requirements:
20 - type:  classad
   requirement:  'Arch=="Intel"'
22 brooklyn.config:
   wars.root:  http://example.cloudlightning.io/webapp/webapp.war
24 http.port:  9280+
   proxy.http.port:  9210+
26 java.sysprops:
   cloudlightning.example.ray.url:
28         $brooklyn:formatString("drmaa://%s",
                 component("RaytracingApplicationId").
30               attributeWhenReady("drmaa.url"))
```

Listing 4.3 An Abstract Blueprint

provide the required information (the **cloudlightning.entity.meta. RaytracingApp** type is not known to Brooklyn).

This service is handled by the CloudLightning SDE by interpreting the provided application information (in this case, the type) and the corresponding matching information. The information needed for the normal SDE operation is defined at the service level, under the **cloudlightning. config** attribute.

The relevant attributes handled by the SDE at the "service-requirements" level are:

- *Type*: this field defines the syntax used for expressing this requirement. Currently the only defined syntax is based on the ClassAds system[4].

- *Requirements*: this field defines the expression interpreted by the SOSM system to identify the appropriate resource required for this service.
- *Rank*: this field defines the way of ranking the possible solutions obtained from the underlying SOSM infrastructure; this expression might be used to prefer resources by various attributes, eventually based on power consumption or computing power.

The "requirements" attribute is aimed at restricting the resources that the SOSM subsystem can consider for choosing the proper implementation for the user-requested service. This attribute is expected to be used by HPC application to express their performance requirements, and it is complemented by the "rank" attribute, used for expressing preference regarding the available and matching resources.

4.6.3   CloudLightning Blueprint

The CloudLightning Blueprint represents the outcome of the Service Decomposition Operation and basically represents a fully qualified Blueprint document that can be handled by the CAMP framework (in our case, Brooklyn).

As seen in Listing 4.4, all "abstract" specifications have been replaced with concrete ones. For example, the **cloudlightning.entity.meta. RaytracingApp** type has been replaced with another type understood by Brooklyn (**cloudlightning.entity.impl.HPCCluster**). This new type is complemented by a new set of attributes that provide deployment-specific information.

It is important to note that the "location" attribute has been customised to provide CloudLightning-specific information; particularly in this case, it contains a handle provided by the underlying SOSM subsystem that can be used at deployment time for synchronising information between the various subsystems. Notice that the **cloudlightning.entity. impl.HPCCluster** is known to Brooklyn due to the fact that it is registered by the EAO in the corresponding catalogue.

4.7   EXAMPLE OF APPLICATION CREATION
AND DEPLOYMENT

The architecture of the CloudLightning Gateway Service was presented previously in Sect. 4.5. This section demonstrates, using an example of a raytracing application, the ease with which the application topology can be created and deployed using the CloudLightning Gateway Service. This

```
 id: jetty-node-with-raytracing-compute
2 name: "Web␣Application␣With␣Raytracing␣Computing␣Resource"
 origin: http://cloudlightning.io/
4 locations:
 - cloudlightning-openstack
6 services:
 - type: cloudlightning.entity.impl.HPCCluster
8 name: RaytracingApplicationId
 location:
10 cloudlightning-openstack:
 session:handle: "b4cfc054-b760-4d82-a2ce-96a65b3d72d0"
12 brooklyn.config:
 cloudlightning.deployment:
14 puppet.manifests.location: "http://p.cloudlightning.io/m/intelphicluster"
 - type: brooklyn.entity.webapp.ControlledDynamicWebAppCluster
16 name: webApp
 location:
18 cloudlightning-openstack:
 session:handle: "26670286-a0ad-499e-9fef-f665d156e27e"
20 brooklyn.config:
 wars.root: http://example.cloudlightning.io/
22         webapp/webapp.war
 http.port: 9280+
24 proxy.http.port: 9210+
 java.sysprops:
26 cloudlightning.example.ray.url:
         $brooklyn:formatString("drmaa://%s",
28             component("RaytracingApplicationId").
             attributeWhenReady("drmaa.url"))
```

Listing 4.4   The CloudLightning Blueprint

use case is used to illustrate a user's interactions with the Gateway Service, enhancing the resource optimisation feature. The remainder of this section provides a brief overview of the steps to be taken to safely create, optimise, and deploy the raytracing application on the CloudLightning environment. Some of the essential steps are also depicted in screenshots taken from the actual system.

The process is as follows:

Step 1:   To initialise the system, start Alien4Cloud service.

Step 2:   Add the plugin to the desired orchestrator (CloudLightning uses Brooklyn-TOSCA as the underlying orchestrator). After the plugin is loaded, Alien4Cloud will present the orchestrator in the list of available plugins.

Step 3:   Create a new orchestrator from the UI and link it to the newly added plugin.

Step 5:   Before one can connect the orchestrator instance from Alien4Cloud to the underlying orchestrator (basically, the SOSM subsystem), one has to ensure that the Gateway Service Orchestrator is running. This step is not a mandatory step to be taken but it is advised.

Step 6:   From the web console one can connect to the bespoke orchestrator. Before any further steps can be taken, wait until the orchestrator state is CONNECTED.

Step 7:   After the orchestrator is connected, download the CSAR archive from a remote *git* repository.[5]

The orchestrator comes with *git* integration functionalities, and the only requirement is to have stored all custom CSAR files in such a repository. In case of the raytracing example, one has to enter the predefined *git* credentials and URL. The download process of the CSAR archive starts only after one clicks the Import button.

Step 8:   Add the CloudLightning plugin to have access to the CloudLightning functionalities.

Step 9:   For the creation of new applications one has to use the functionalities exposed by Alien4Cloud, more precisely the New Application panel. The CSAR archive may contain already defined application templates, and one can select some of those for the intended application design.

Step 10:   As soon as the application creation step is finished, one can view the design and application in its home panel.

Step 11:   The previously defined topology contains four types of nodes, which can be viewed in the Topology tab (see Fig. 4.10). It is also possible to view the newly created topology in YAML format by pressing the YAML tab in the designer.

Step 12:   Next, enter the CloudLightning Optimisation Panel and start the optimisation process from the SOSM Optimiser button (see Fig. 4.11). On the left-hand side, one can view the endpoint for the SDE.

Step 13:   Check that the SDE is up and running, and when the optimisation process is finished, one can notice that the abstract nodes have been replaced with concrete ones also in the application designer.

Step 14:   As a final step prepare for the deployment of application by entering into the Deployment Panel. The orchestrator has already sent information about locations to Alien4Cloud and one has only to select the desired location.

Step 15:   By moving to Deploy tab one can trigger the actual deployment of the application. This step is performed by pressing the Deploy button and wait until it finishes. Once pressed one can follow the explicit progress of the deployment also in the orchestrator console.

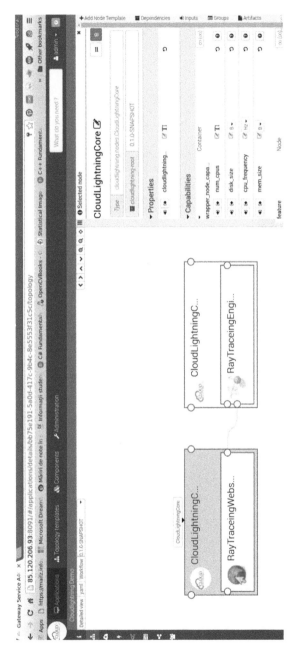

Fig. 4.10 Application topology: CloudLightning Core 1 node

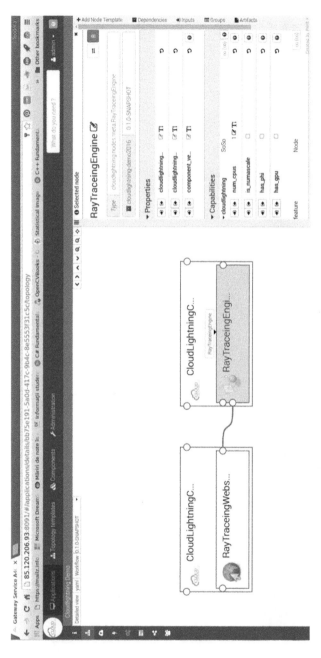

Fig. 4.11 Start of the optimisation process

4.8   Conclusion

This chapter presented the CloudLightning Gateway Service, a user-friendly interface that enables users to create and deploy applications with minimum knowledge regarding the resource selection process. The Gateway Service is a key component of the CloudLightning system that facilitates application lifecycle management in the context of a cloud environment. Users can design the application topology using the *Drag & Drop* mechanism of the Gateway Service UI and link together the components of their application. From here, the topology is sent to the *SDE*, which is responsible for interacting with the *SOSM* system. The SDE translates the information from the application topology, into a specific CloudLightning Blueprint, using the *CloudLightning Service Description Language*. Next, *SOSM* handles the resource discovery process, assigning the most suitable set of resources for a user application, based on the received CloudLightning blueprint. In the following step, the *SOSM* sends back to the *SDE* a CloudLightning blueprint, with a proposed resource for each component of the application topology. In the end, the user may review the final version of its application topology, with the assigned resources, and start the process of application deployment.

4.9   Chapter 4 Related CloudLightning Readings

1. Dragan, I., Fortis, T. F., & Neagul, M. (2016). Exposing HPC services in the cloud: The CloudLightning approach. *Scalable Computing: Practice and Experience, 17*(4), 323–330.
2. Selea, T., Dragan, I., & Fortiş, T. F. (2017, April). The CloudLightning approach to cloud-user interaction. In *Proceedings of the 1st International Workshop on Next generation of Cloud Architectures*, Vol. 4, ACM.

Notes

1. The term CAMP provider is used in the sense as defined by the CAMP specification, basically "an implementation of the service aspects of this specification."
2. Abstract Blueprints are those blueprints that will be later on filled with concrete resources by the CL-System.
3. https://brooklyn.apache.org/learnmore/theory.html
4. https://research.cs.wisc.edu/htcondor/classad/classad.html
5. One keeps definitions of services in CSAR format in a remote repository.

References

Apache Software Foundation. (n.d.). Apache Brooklyn. Retrieved October 15, 2017, from https://brooklyn.apache.org/

Apache Software Foundation. (n.d.). Apache jClouds®. Retrieved October 15, 2017, from https://jclouds.apache.org/start

Breiter, G., Leymann, F., & Spatzier, T. (2012, May). *Topology and orchestration specification for cloud applications (TOSCA): Cloud service archive (CSAR).* International Business Machines Corporation.

Carlson, M., Chapman, M., Heneveld, A., Hinkelman, S., Johnston-Watt, D., Karmarkar, A., et al. (2012). OASIS, Tech. Rep. *Cloud Application Management for Platforms.* Retrieved October 10, 2017, from http://cloudspecs.org/CAMP/CAMP_v1-0.pdf

Dragan, I., Selea, T., & Fortis, T.-F. (2017). *D5.2.1 Gateway Service.* CloudLightning consortium. Retrieved October 15, 2017, from.

Morrison, J., Xiong, H., Dong, D., & Momani, B. (2016). *D3.1.2 Architecture.* CloudLightning Consortium. Retrieved October 15, 2017, from.

Neagul, M., Dragan, I., & Craciun, C. (2016). *D4.1.1 protocol specification and API.* CloudLightning Consortium. Retrieved October 15, 2017, from.

OASIS Open. (2013). *Topology and orchestration specification for cloud applications version 1.0.* Retrieved October 10, 2017, from http://docs.oasis-open.org/tosca/TOSCA/v1.0/os/TOSCA-v1.0-os.html

Openstack.org. (2017). OpenStack Mistral. Retrieved October 18, 2017, from https://docs.openstack.org/mistral/latest/

Openstack.org. OpenStack Solum. Retrieved October 18, 2017, from https://docs.openstack.org/solum/latest/

Openstack.org. Heat—OpenStack. Retrieved October 15, 2017, from https://docs.openstack.org/heat/pike/

Solomon, M. (2003). *The ClassAd Language Reference Manual, Version 2.1.* Computer Sciences Department, University of Wisconsin, Madison, WI, USA.

Sun, L., Dong, H., & Ashraf, J. (2012, October). Survey of service description languages and their issues in cloud computing. In *Eighth International Conference on Semantics, Knowledge and Grids (SKG)* (pp. 128–135). IEEE.

Xiong, H., Dong, D., Morrison, J., Antoniadis, I., Neagul, M., Giannoutakis, K., et al. (2016). *D5.1.1 service description format.* CloudLightning Consortium. Retrieved 15 October, 2017, from https://cloudlightning.eu/blog/service-description-format/d5-1-1-service-description-format-3/

CHAPTER 5

Simulating Heterogeneous Clouds at Scale

Christos K. Filelis-Papadopoulos,
Konstantinos M. Giannoutakis, George A. Gravvanis,
Charalampos S. Kouzinopoulos, Antonios T. Makaratzis,
and Dimitrios Tzovaras

Abstract In this chapter, a review of existing cloud simulation frame-works is given along with an overview of the recently proposed CloudLightning simulation framework. Moreover, the parallel architecture and parallel implementation details of the CloudLightning simulator are presented along with the characteristics of the supported cloud architectures. These architectures include the traditional centralised approach as well as the Self-Organised and Self-Managed CloudLightning approach. The supported memory, network, and application execution models are

C. K. Filelis-Papadopoulos (✉) • G. A. Gravvanis
Democritus University of Thrace, Komotini, Greece
e-mail: cpapad@ee.duth.gr; ggravvan@ee.duth.gr

K. M. Giannoutakis • C. S. Kouzinopoulos • A. T. Makaratzis • D. Tzovaras
Centre for Research and Technology Hellas, Thessaloniki, Greece
e-mail: kgiannou@iti.gr; kouzinopoulos@iti.gr; antomaka@iti.gr; Dimitrios.
Tzovaras@iti.gr

© The Author(s) 2018   119
T. Lynn et al. (eds.), *Heterogeneity, High Performance Computing,*
Self-Organization and the Cloud, Palgrave Studies in Digital
Business & Enabling Technologies,
https://doi.org/10.1007/978-3-319-76038-4_5

reviewed. Furthermore, a recently proposed class of power models for heterogeneous CPU-Accelerator-based hardware is discussed. Finally, large-scale simulations for traditional and Self-Organised and Self-Managed cloud environments are presented and compared.

Keywords CloudLightning simulator • Self-organisation • Self-management • Scalability • Large-scale simulations

5.1   INTRODUCTION

Cloud simulation tools have been extensively used for the analysis of cloud data centres, since the cost of experimentation using various scenarios is low. A number of different aspects, related to cloud environments, can be studied through simulation including resource allocation strategies, live migration of running applications to more efficient data centre resources, energy consumption, and hardware resource utilisation. Several cloud simulation tools have been developed during the past few years focusing on different aspects of cloud environments. These tools can be categorised into:

- *Discrete Event Simulators (DES)*: These examine macro-scale phenomena, such as application events that take place in certain moments in time while completely disregarding micro-scale phenomena, including network packet communication. DES are used to examine large-scale simulations, while focus is given among others in the study of cloud environments behaviour in terms of service delivery, Virtual Machine (VM) allocation policies, utilisation of resources, and the energy consumption of data centres.
- *Packet-Level Simulators (PLS)*: These examine micro-scale phenomena related to cloud environments, including packet loss and network communication protocols. PLS offer high levels of accuracy at the cost of performance though, since large-scale data centres cannot be studied due to the restricting resolution of the simulations.

Cloud infrastructures continue to grow in both size and diversity to cater for demand in terms of both user and data volumes and the variety of hardware resources. As a result, existing cloud simulation tools cannot be used to efficiently simulate these heterogeneous environments at scales several orders of magnitude greater than traditional data centres. By 2020, hyperscale data centres will account for a substantial portion of all cloud workloads and data (Cisco 2016). Furthermore, as hyperscale data centres consist of servers in distinct geographical locations, the efficient management of such infrastructures is made more difficult resulting in network congestion and underutilisation of resources. Resource heterogeneity further exacerbates these challenges. While hyperscale data centre operators increasingly offer specialised hardware, such as Graphical Processing Units (GPUs), Many Integrated Cores (MICs), and Field-Programmable Gate Arrays (FPGAs), existing cloud simulation tools do not support them. The efficient exploitation of the hardware infrastructure of heterogeneous hyperscale cloud environments is a topic of great importance during the last few years; thus, cloud simulation tools for studying heterogeneous cloud environments that can cater for hyperscale need to be developed.

The remainder of this chapter is organised as follows. Section 5.2 provides a summary review of common cloud simulation frameworks used by the scientific community and their limitations. A new simulation framework, the CloudLightning Simulator, designed to simulate hyperscale cloud environments composed of heterogeneous resources is presented in Sect. 5.3. This is followed by a discussion of initial experimentation using the CloudLightning Simulator to compare service delivery of three application scenarios: oil and gas exploration, ray tracing, and genomics, using (i) conventional cloud service delivery and (ii) cloud service delivery using a self-organising self-managing (SOSM) approach.

5.2   CLOUD SIMULATION FRAMEWORKS

During the last decade, various cloud simulation frameworks have been proposed, such as CloudSim (Calheiros et al. 2011), DCSim (Tighe et al. 2012), GDCSim (Gupta et al. 2011), GreenCloud (Kliazovich et al. 2012), iCanCloud (Nunez et al. 2012), and CloudSched (Tian et al. 2015). However, no existing cloud simulation framework is designed for hyperscale simulations.

One of the main limitations of existing cloud simulation tools is the lack of scalability. Most existing cloud simulation tools do not support parallelism; thus, the simulation of very large data centres is not possible (Byrne et al. 2017). Parallelism is of great importance for the simulation of hyperscale cloud environments since both computational work and memory requirements can be distributed among multiple nodes, reducing the execution time significantly and enabling the simulation of large-scale data centres.

An important factor influencing scalability of the extant simulation tools is memory requirements. In DES a large number of events should be created and retained. The number of these events is closely related to the number of resources simulated as well as the input tasks. Discrete Event based simulators initialise the task list that will be executed for the whole simulation and augment it gradually with new events according to time. This process requires retaining a very large list in memory, its augmentation with new events, and its sorting in order to perform events in the correct order. Thus, memory requirements increase significantly with the number of resources or the simulation time. Memory restrictions also occur due to the high level of detail of the simulated components, such as in the case of the iCanCloud and GreenCloud frameworks, which becomes prohibiting in very large-scale executions.

The effective management of resources is a significant challenge as their number increases. More specifically, strategies which require the detection of specific hardware cannot be applied or require significant computational cost when hyperscale systems are considered. Also, status information corresponding to the underlying hardware resources is becoming outdated, and thus efficient management of the system becomes more challenging. Specialised strategies are required in hyperscale cloud environments for the efficient and up-to-date management of the system. Such strategies are not supported in existing simulation frameworks, and thus the simulation of hyperscale systems is difficult to perform.

Finally, the inclusion of heterogeneous resources is not supported by existing cloud simulation tools. Simple generic models are required for the simulation of heterogeneous resources in order to be integrated in cloud simulation environments (Makaratzis et al. 2017; Giannoutakis et al. 2017).

5.3   CloudLightning Simulator

Unlike existing frameworks, the CloudLightning Simulator has been designed from the ground up as a massively scalable solution, able to simulate hyperscale data centres consisting of millions of cloud nodes/servers.

The framework is written in C++ and is parallelised using Message Passing Interface (MPI) (Gropp et al. 1996) and OpenMP (Dagum and Menon 1998) to enable the efficient handling of hyperscale simulations. CloudLightning supports the simulation of heterogeneous infrastructures (including GPUs, MICs, and FPGAs/DFEs) that are commonly used for the acceleration of High Performance Computing applications. One important characteristic of the developed framework is the use of a time-advancing loop, a technique that removes the need for pre-computation and storage of future events, resulting in a significant reduction of its memory requirements. This allows the integration of dynamic resource allocation policies, such as SOSM, enabling the efficient management of computer resources for simulating hyperscale environments. Moreover, the CloudLightning Simulator places an emphasis on the simplicity of the models it uses, focusing on models that require reduced number of computations for producing the results of the simulations without loss of accuracy. Finally, all inputs and outputs of the simulator are represented graphically.

The remainder of this section presents the generalised and extensible CloudLightning simulation framework for simulating heterogeneous resources using an SOSM approach.

5.3.1   *Architecture and Basic Characteristics of the Parallel CloudLightning Simulation Framework*

The CloudLightning Simulator was designed to simulate clouds relying on the Warehouse Scale Computer (WSC) architecture (Barroso et al. 2013). WSC has been adopted by a multitude of companies including Google, Amazon, Yahoo, Microsoft, and Apple, and has been widely used in the design of cloud environments (Mars 2012). In the WSC architecture, interconnected cloud computing nodes are grouped into cells that are centrally managed (Fig. 5.1).

In this architecture, the Gateway service is responsible for redirecting end user requests to the appropriate Cells. The Gateway service is the entry point of the system and is a cloud entity that receives resource requests from the end users and redirects them to the Cells. A conceptual cloud architecture with multiple Cells is presented in Fig. 5.2. The resources are organised and monitored by the Cell manager's broker that is responsible for the provision of appropriate resources to end user

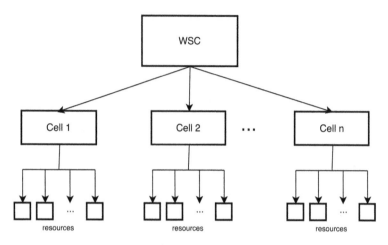

Fig. 5.1 Warehouse Scale Computer abstract architecture

requests and for the deployment of incoming tasks to the available resources. The broker component is composed of multiple services, including orchestration, telemetry, and identity service. Hyperscale cloud environments consist of a considerably large number of Cells.

In the CloudLightning simulation framework, each Cell is hosted on a different computing node of a distributed system, while the Gateway service is hosted on the master computing node. The communication between the Gateway service and the Cells is performed using the MPI framework. The following operations are performed by each Cell (Filelis-Papadopoulos et al. 2017, b):

- Receiving simulation parameters
- Initialisation of different components, including hardware resources, the broker, network, telemetry, and the SOSM engine
- Receiving the task queue in each time-step
- Searching for available resources for the execution of the tasks, using the SOSM engine
- Updating the state of the resources and controlling the execution of the tasks
- Communicating status information to the Gateway Service

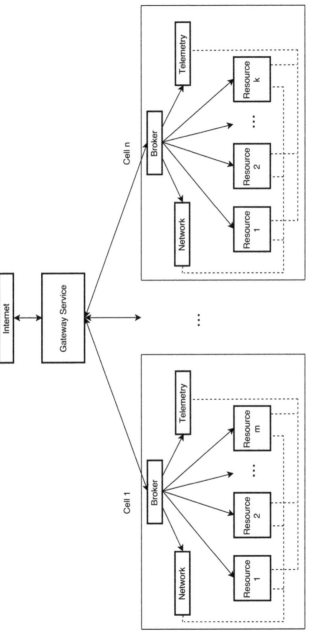

Fig. 5.2   Abstract cloud architecture with multiple cells

The operations performed by the Gateway service are the following (Filelis-Papadopoulos et al. 2017, b):

- Retaining simulation inputs and communicating data to the Cells for the initialisation of the simulation components
- Creation of the task queue in each time moment, fragmentation of the task queue into subqueues, and communication of the subqueues to the Cells, by maintaining load balance through all Cells
- Receiving status information from the Cells
- Processing and storing historical statistics and metrics

The parallelisation of the CloudLightning Simulator in distributed systems is of great importance, since simulating hyperscale infrastructures is a computationally and memory-intensive process. For this reason, various components of the CloudLightning Simulator use the OpenMP framework in different ways to accelerate their computations on shared memory multiprocessors. The Gateway Service processes statistics in parallel—the Cells perform resource discovery and task deployment as well as the update of the resources' state on different multiprocessor cores. The SOSM techniques are also performed in parallel.

Figure 5.3 presents the software architecture of the CloudLightning Simulator (Filelis-Papadopoulos et al. 2017):

5.3.2   SOSM Engine

One of the most important characteristics of the CloudLightning Simulator is the use of SOSM techniques to control the underlying resources of the Cells in a more efficient manner (Filelis-Papadopoulos et al. 2017).

In traditional cloud architectures, the resources are managed by the broker, a central entity that is responsible for the search and deployment of the available resources with respect to incoming task requests, the collection of data for the state of all underlying resources, and the management of all underlying resources of the data centre. This centralised approach has limitations due to the computational complexity involved in locating specific hardware, especially when the number of resources increases. Locating the most appropriate server for the execution of a task is a computationally expensive operation in large data centres, and it is generally avoided in favour of strategies such as the "first-fit approach," where a task is deployed on the first available server or coalition of servers.

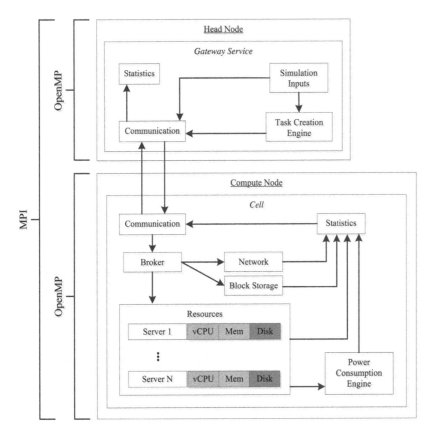

Fig. 5.3 Software architecture of the parallel CloudLightning simulation framework

This type of strategy is not effective though in terms of both computational and energy efficiency, resulting largely in the underutilisation of the available resources (Filelis-Papadopoulos et al. 2017). More effective strategies, such as SOSM, need to be applied to achieve high levels of resource utilisation and thus computational and energy efficiency.

In the CloudLightning architecture, each Cell is organised in a hierarchical tree structure. As discussed earlier, the tree contains different entities, including prescription Routers (pRouters), prescription Switches (pSwitches), and virtual Rack Managers (vRMs). Figure 5.4 presents an example of the CloudLightning tree structure. In this structure, the

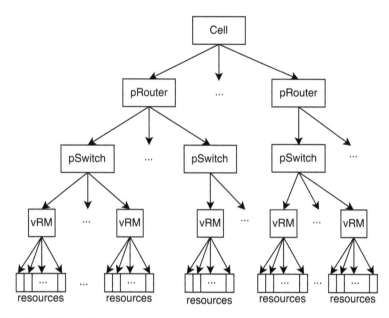

Fig. 5.4 Hierarchical structure of the SOSM engine

resources are locally managed by the vRMs which in turn are locally managed by the pSwitches, while the pSwitches are locally managed by the pRouters. The local management of the architectural components allows the efficient collection and analysis of data that can lead to an improved decision-making process. Each component can describe the state of its underlying resources since metrics describing the state of the resources are collected with respect to an interval and averaged by each component to form its own state. Also, weights describing the desired state of the system are communicated from the Gateway Service to the underlying components. By using these metrics and weights, each component's Suitability Index is computed. The Suitability Index expresses how appropriate is a component to receive an incoming task. By using the Suitability Index, each incoming task can be subsequently directed to the most efficient resources.

The exchange of metrics and weights between the components is part of the Self-Management actions and is performed by all the components of the SOSM engine. The Self-Organisation techniques, on the other hand, are solely performed by the vRMs and the pSwitches. In the case of vRMs, there can be an exchange of resources between vRMs that are hosted by the same pSwitch, in order to maximise the efficiency of the system and to host tasks that require more resources than available on a vRM. New vRMs can also be created, while vRMs that do not contain any resources to manage can be destroyed. Similarly, pSwitches that are hosted by the same pRouter can exchange vRMs; new pSwitches can be created, while existing pSwitches can be dismissed when they have no vRMs to manage.

Each pRouter of a Cell is homogeneous, as it contains resources of the same type. In order to maintain the homogeneity, Self-Organising actions are not performed at the pRouter level; thus, pSwitches cannot be exchanged between pRouters. For this reason, pRouters are the entry point for the selection of a specific type of resource inside a Cell (Filelis-Papadopoulos et al. 2017).

The SOSM system improves significantly the scalability of cloud environments since the most appropriate hardware for the execution of a task can be located fast and with low computational cost, even in data centres with a very large number of resources. In the CloudLightning Simulator, the SOSM engine is implemented in parallel using the OpenMP framework.

5.3.2.1 Power Consumption Modelling

To estimate the power consumption of large-scale heterogeneous data centres, a number of different power models for both Central Processing Unit (CPU) servers and combined CPU-accelerator pairs were developed. The power models are generic with low computational cost (Filelis-Papadopoulos et al. 2017; Giannoutakis et al. 2017). For this reason, the CloudLightning Simulator is capable of computing the power consumption of very large heterogeneous data centres without a significant impact on its scalability. The following subsection gives a detailed presentation of the integrated power consumption models.

CPU Power Models

Piecewise interpolation methods between recorded CPU power consumption levels, and generic models that estimate the trend of the power-utilisation diagram of CPUs by using the idle and maximum power consumption of the CPU servers, have been integrated.

The interpolation methods are performed between recorded CPU power consumption levels that are available mainly as part of the

Standard Performance Evaluation Corporation (SPEC) benchmark (SPEC 2008). Existing simulators, such as CloudSim, use linear interpolation between power measurements on rounded utilisation intervals (i.e. 0%, 10%, 20%, etc.) (Beloglazov and Buyya 2012). In order to achieve improved accuracy, the interpolation methods in the CloudLightning Simulator are applied on the exact utilisation intervals of the power measurements (i.e. 0%, 10.2%, 19.7%, etc.) as the error of the rounded interpolation intervals increases when simulating very large data centres (Giannoutakis et al. 2017). Two different interpolation methods were used, the linear and the "not-a-knot" cubic spline interpolation.

Generic models were also integrated, since they require less computational cost and power measurements compared to the interpolation methods. The models estimate the power consumption of CPU servers by using the utilisation of the CPU server and its power consumption in idle and max states. The linear, square, cubic, and square root models that have been used in existing cloud simulators (i.e. CloudSim) were integrated (Beloglazov and Buyya 2012). For the CloudLightning Simulator, a generic CPU power model was used based on a third-degree polynomial, which estimates more accurately the trend of the power-utilisation diagram of CPU servers (Filelis-Papadopoulos et al. 2017). The trend of the generic models compared with the actual CPU measurements provided by SPEC (SPEC 2008) for an HP Proliant DL560 Gen 9[1] is presented in Fig. 5.5.

Existing cloud simulators (i.e. GreenCloud and CloudSim) support the use of real application traces in order to compute the power consumption of the simulated applications in each time-step. This approach would negatively affect the scalability of the simulator in large-scale simulations, and for this reason, mean values of real application traces were computed and integrated. More specifically, the mean value of the CPU utilisation for each application is used to compute the mean power consumption of the application. Then, the energy consumption of the application is computed by multiplying the mean power consumption of the application with its execution time. This approach provides a lower computational cost, while the result of the energy consumption of the application is computed with approximately the same accuracy that would have been obtained if all the power traces were used. This methodology has been tested, achieving high levels of accuracy in the estimation of the energy consumption of applications (Makaratzis et al. 2017).

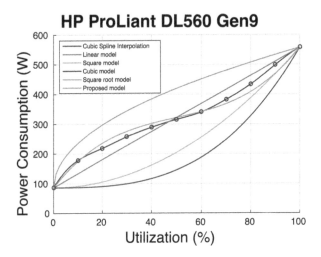

Fig. 5.5   Generic CPU power models compared to the power-utilisation diagram of an HP Proliant DL560 Gen 9 server

Combined CPU-Accelerator Power Models

A generic power consumption model was used for the estimation of the power consumption of accelerators such as GPUs, MICs, and DFE (Giannoutakis et al. 2017). This model was built around the idea that the maximum power consumption of an accelerator is consumed when an application is executed on the accelerator, while the idle power consumption is consumed when the application is executed only on the CPU. This binary model provides simplicity and increased accuracy (Makaratzis et al. 2017). The model for the power consumption of hardware accelerators is described as follows:

$$P_{acc}(\rho) = (1-\rho)P_{acc-min} + \rho P_{acc-max}$$

where $P_{acc-min}$ and $P_{acc-max}$ are the minimum and maximum power consumption values, respectively, that the application can consume on the accelerator, while ρ is the percentage of the application that is parallelised on the accelerator, thus in each time moment. Similarly, with the utilisation parameters of the CPU power model, the mean value of parameter is computed based on real application traces, thus the mean value of the power that is consumed on the accelerator is computed for the total execution time of the application. The combined CPU-accelerator mean power consumption of the application is computed as the sum of the mean power consumption of the CPU server and the mean power consumption of the accelerator. The energy consumption of an application that is executed on a heterogeneous node is computed by multiplying the combined CPU-accelerator mean power consumption with the execution time of the application.

To conclude, in order to keep the computational cost low, generic CPU and accelerator power models were integrated in the CloudLightning Simulator. The simplicity of the models is of great importance since models that are based on architectural details of the hardware resources require a substantial number of computations, considering the heterogeneity and the very large number of resources in the simulations. These models were validated on heterogeneous testbeds and a good accuracy level was achieved (Makaratzis et al. 2017).

5.3.2.2 Memory, Storage, and Network Modelling

Detailed modelling of memory would negatively affect the scalability of the simulator, especially in large-scale simulations, since it would require an increased amount of computations. Memory was implemented as a resource, measured in GBytes, that is used in the allocation of VMs to physical servers. Memory overcommitment was also implemented; thus, the total available memory was computed as the product of the total physical memory and the overcommitment ratio. The power consumption of memory was included in the power consumption of the CPU servers, eliminating the need for a separate memory power consumption calculation.

The modelling of storage was also implemented with simplicity in order to keep the computational cost in low levels. The storage was implemented as a resource measured in TBytes. Global storage was not implemented, though its impact can be added directly to the time span of tasks. Detailed modelling of the power consumption of storage was not implemented since it would require substantially large number of computations, which would negatively affect the scalability of the simulator. The energy consumption of storage is considered to be included in the energy consumption of the CPU servers, similar to memory modelling.

The network was implemented as a global component, visible from all the underlying resources, with the network bandwidth being shared among the arriving tasks of the system. When the requested network bandwidth exceeds the available capacity, the execution of applications is affected negatively (in terms of the execution time). It should be noted that the network model of the CloudLightning Simulator was implemented through a catalogue of tasks, retaining all tasks executing at a given time-step. A linear model for computing the time required to transfer initial data and output data was implemented with a function of the following form:

$$NT(t) = fileSize / bandwidth$$

where *fileSize* is the size of the file to be transferred and *bandwidth* is the available physical bandwidth.

5.3.2.3 Application Models

In the design of the CloudLightning Simulator, the execution of VMs is part of a given task and their life cycle is directly connected to it. Each task is defined based on the following characteristics (Filelis-Papadopoulos et al. 2017):

- Type of application (Genomics, Oil and Gas, Ray Tracing)
- Available implementations (CPU-only, CPU+GPU, CPU+DFE, CPU+MIC)
- Number of instructions (in Millions of Instructions [MIs])
- Required number of VMs
- Required number of processing units per VM
- Required memory per VM (in GBytes)
- Required storage per VM (in TBytes)
- Required accelerators per VM
- Required network bandwidth

The minimum and maximum values are defined for the actual utilisation of the CPU, the memory, and the network. The actual resources used by an application (utilisation) are computed based on application traces as a percentage of the requested resources over a number of predefined intervals. These utilisation parameters are considered as mean values with respect to the total execution time of the application. This approach maintains the computational cost low, while the desired metrics are obtained with the same accuracy that would have been obtained if all the application traces were used.

All task parameters, including the number of instructions, the required number of VMs, and memory size, are randomly generated using a uniform random number generator with respect to predefined intervals. The intervals are computed based on real application characteristics.

This approach of application modelling reduces computational cost, allowing for large-scale simulations, while also providing realistic results during the simulations.

5.3.2.4 Execution Models

Existing cloud simulators generally create *a priori* task lists for the whole duration of the simulation, augment, and sort that list with respect to events triggered by inputs and so on. However, this has the disadvantage of simulation data storage, not only for the current event but also for future ones, restricting the execution of large-scale simulations over long time periods. In contrast, the CloudLightning Simulator is based on a time-advancing loop, where incoming tasks are created dynamically in each time-step and where each time-step is independent from any previous or future ones (Filelis-Papadopoulos et al. 2017). A task list is then created at the beginning of each time-step, removing the need for data storage of future tasks of the simulation. Creating task lists per time-step reduces significantly the memory requirements of the simulation and offers the ability to simulate dynamical components that change their state according to dynamic strategies, including pRouters, pSwitches, and vRMs while allowing for the simulation over extended time periods.

In the execution of tasks, the time-step is used as the control mechanism of the execution. The performance of applications is measured in MIs while the computational capability of the physical servers is measured in Millions of Instructions per Second (MIPS). In each time-step, the number of instructions that can be executed by the available resources is subtracted from the total number of instructions of the application. This time-step-controlled execution model offers significant capabilities since the impact of various phenomena can be modelled by applying penalties on the execution of tasks. For example, phenomena such as performance degradation due to cache sharing or "noisy-neighbours" can be modelled by reducing the computational capability, meaning that fewer of the application's instructions will be executed on the current time-step. Similarly, the usage of hardware with a higher computational capability, that is, accelerators, can be modelled by increasing the computational capability of the current time-step. Service-level Agreement violations concerning memory, storage, or network limitations can be modelled by applying similar penalties in the execution of tasks.

This approach of execution modelling allows the integration of possible extensions on the simulator, since any phenomenon can be modelled during a simulation by applying penalties or gains in the execution of the applications. Also, this execution model allows the simulation of very large time periods and millions of cloud servers, since the memory requirements of the execution model are very low.

5.4   Experimental Results

This section presents the experimentation framework and the numerical results occurred after simulating the traditional cloud delivery system and the SOSM framework.

The experiments were performed on a cluster consisting of four Dell PowerEdge C4130 nodes, each containing two 10-core Intel Xeon E5-2630 v4 CPUs running at 2.20 GHz (3.10 GHz Max Turbo frequency) with 128GB of Random Access Memory (RAM), and a Dell PowerEdge R730 node containing two 8-core Intel Xeon E5-2609 v4 CPUs running at 1.70 GHz. During the simulation, the Dell PowerEdge R730 node was used to host the Gateway service, while the 4 Dell PowerEdge C4130 nodes were used to host the Cells.

The time period of the simulation was set to one week (604,800 seconds), with a time-step of 1 second. The update interval of the Gateway Service was chosen to be 200 seconds, while the update interval of the pRouters, pSwitches, and vRMs was 20 seconds. The cloud nodes of the simulated data centre were selected to use an Intel Xeon E5-2699 v4 2.20 GHz-based node with 44 cores and 385,063.42 MIPS, 128 GBytes of RAM, and 40 TBytes of storage.

Each Cell consisted of four different types of hardware, that is, CPUs+GPUs, CPUs+MICs, CPUs+DFEs, or CPU servers with no accelerators. Each heterogeneous node consisted of a CPU and four accelerators. The characteristics of the CPUs and the accelerators are presented in Table 5.1. It is noted that the linear interpolation method on uneven utilisation intervals was used for the estimation of the power consumption of the CPU servers, where the power values for the various utilisation intervals were obtained[2] from SPEC (SPEC 2008).

Table 5.1 Selected simulation framework characteristics (adapted from Byrne et al. 2017)

Simulation platform	Licence	Language(s)	Platform portability	Distributed architecture	Model persistence type	Web API availability	GUI availability	Headless execution	Result output format
CloudSched	–	Java	Yes	No	Text	No	Yes	No	XLS, Text
CloudSim	Apache 2	Java	Yes	No	YAML	No	No	Yes	Text
DCSim	GPL 3	Java	Yes	No	Java classes	No	No	Yes	Text
GDCSim	GPL 2	C/C++, Shell	No	No	C code	No	No	Yes	Text
GreenCloud	GPL	C++, TCL, JS, CSS, Shell	No	No	TCL	Yes	Yes	Yes	Dashboard plots
iCanCloud	GPL 3, GNU, Academic	C/C++, Shell	Yes	No	NED	No	Yes	Yes	Text

During the simulations, three different types of applications were considered. The characteristics of the applications are presented in Tables 5.2 and 5.3.

The CloudLightning Simulator was executed for different number of resources, Cells, and submitted tasks. Each Cell was hosted on a Dell PowerEdge C4130 node, while in the experiments with eight Cells, each computing node was hosting two Cells. Three different configurations were tested. In the first configuration, 11,000 resources per Cell were utilised, while the experiment was performed for different number of Cells. Similarly, in the second configuration, 110,000 resources per Cell were used, and in the third configuration, 1,100,000 resources per Cell were considered. The maximum number of submitted tasks was set equal to four per second when one Cell was used, while this number was multiplied with the number of Cells when additional Cells were used. The VM allocation policy used was the "first-fit approach," according to which tasks are placed on the first available server found.

Table 5.2 Hardware characteristics

Hardware	MIPS	Idle power consumption (Watts)	Max power consumption (Watts)
CPU	385,063.4268	44.9	269.0
MIC	1,347,721.9938	30.0	350.0
DFE	2,310,380.5608	70.0	100.0
GPU	1,155,190.2804	50.0	400.0

Table 5.3 Application characteristics

Application type:	1	2	3
Millions of instructions	1386.23–5544.91	462.08–2772.46	693.11–4158.69
Number of VMs	1–16	1–8	1–4
Number of vCPUs	4–8	8–16	4–8
Memory (GBytes)	4–8	4–8	4–8
Storage (TBytes)	0.02–0.04	0.01–0.02	0.04–0.08
Network bandwidth (MBps)	2.5–5	0.5–1	2.5–5
Network storage (GB)	0–0	0–0	0–0
Implementations	1, 2, 3	1, 2, 3	1, 4
ρ	0, 0.7, 0.5	0, 0.8, 0.9	0, 0.9

Table 5.4 presents the outputs, in terms of the number of accepted tasks, the average processor and accelerator utilisation, the average network utilisation, the energy consumption of the data centre, and the execution time of the CloudLightning Simulator, simulating a traditional centralised cloud service delivery system.

For all different configurations, it can be observed that the total number of rejected tasks was high, with an ~86% task rejection on average. The task rejection was caused mainly by the network congestion appearing early in the simulated cloud (Fig. 5.6). Despite the fact that the selection of applications and their corresponding implementations (Table 5.3) were performed randomly using a uniform random generator, accelerator implementations were starting to be rejected after a period of simulated time, since the network resources are shared between the resources hosted across a Cell. This yields the acceptance of additional CPU tasks that in general require more computational time for execution and consequently overload the network.

The energy consumption estimation of the cloud infrastructure increased with the number of resources per Cell and the number of Cells. It is expected that, except from the idle servers that consume the minimum power, when the utilisation of the cloud increases, the energy consumption will proportionally increase.

The CloudLightning Simulator was also tested using the SOSM resource allocation framework, for 100 resources per vRM, 10 vRMs per pSwitch, and 5 pSwitches per pRouter. The VM allocation policy was "Task Compaction," where the system is provisioning as many VMs as possible on each physical server. Table 5.5 presents the outputs of the CloudLightning Simulator, in terms of the number of accepted tasks, the average processor and accelerator utilisation, the average network utilisation, the energy consumption of the data centre, and the execution time of the simulator, when using the SOSM engine.

During the SOSM resource allocation simulation, it can be observed that there was a more balanced utilisation between CPUs and accelerators. More specifically, accelerators tended to be utilised at the same levels as CPUs, while in many cases, their utilisation percentages overcame the corresponding CPU ones. This was due to the fact that the system (SOSM framework) decides the resources (and types of implementations) to be allocated for a task, according to the predefined assessment functions, that targets on (a) improved service delivery, (b) computational efficiency, (c) improved energy consumption, and (d) efficient management of

Table 5.4 Execution of the CloudLightning simulator for different number of resources, different number of Cells, and different number of tasks for the traditional centralised cloud service delivery system

Configuration	Cells	Submitted tasks	Accepted tasks	Average processor utilisation (over active servers)	Average accelerator utilisation (over active servers)	Average network utilisation (%)	Energy consumption (GWh)	Execution time (sec)
Configuration 1: 11,000 resources per Cell	1	2,419,200	136,734	34.15% (89.94%)	1.51% (72.83%)	99.46	0.41434	2037.57
	2	4,838,400	770,219	46.25% (94.23%)	4.78% (64.93%)	96.95	1.25828	2565.49
	3	7,257,600	1,363,382	43.19% (90.71%)	4.48% (56.68%)	98.78	1.72955	2691.67
	4	9,676,800	2,446,410	45.82% (91.59%)	7.19% 77.86%	96.7	2.55623	3004.94
	8	19,353,600	3,301,122	44.05% (91.2%)	4.48% (70.72%)	98.18	4.40216	2833.70
Configuration 2: 110,000 resources per Cell	1	2,419,200	136,578	3.42% (90.03%)	0.15% (71.53%)	99.47	2.15033	5102.79
	2	4,838,400	420,451	5.29% (86.86%)	0.16% (62.15%)	99.39	4.5139	6197.07
	3	7,257,600	1,096,134	4.36% (89.58%)	0.35% (55.5%)	99.26	6.83921	7560.64
	4	9,676,800	1,990,111	7.03% (90.06%)	0.45% (74.8%)	98.85	9.63639	7599.38
	8	19,353,600	2,583,260	4.67% (87.11%)	0.31% (69.21%)	99.07	18.03786	7465.97

(continued)

Table 5.4 (continued)

Configuration	Cells	Submitted tasks	Accepted tasks	Average processor utilisation (over active servers)	Average accelerator utilisation (over active servers)	Average network utilisation (%)	Energy consumption (GWh)	Execution time (sec)
Configuration 3: 1,100,000 resources per Cell	1	2,419,200	136,462	0.34% (89.96%)	0.02% (70.99%)	99.46	19.50804	41,319.31
	2	4,838,400	419,313	0.53% (86.61%)	0.02% (61.93%)	99.39	39.22957	40,754.94
	3	7,257,600	1,095,999	0.44% (89.09%)	0.03% (55.4%)	99.26	58.91502	40,747.46
	4	9,676,800	1,989,893	0.71% (90.05%)	0.05% (75.46%)	98.85	79.07197	44,777.33
	8	19,353,600	2,585,701	0.47% (87.06%)	0.03% (69.36%)	99.07	156.90569	43,971.90

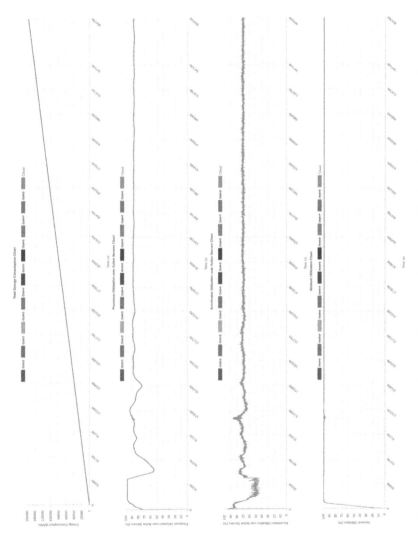

Fig. 5.6 Energy consumption, processor, accelerator, and network utilisation of the cloud over time for the traditional cloud delivery simulation

Table 5.5 Execution of the CloudLightning simulator for different number of resources, different number of Cells, and different number of tasks by using SOSM engine

Configuration	Cells	Submitted tasks	Accepted tasks	Average processor utilisation (over active servers)	Average accelerator utilisation (over active servers)	Average network utilisation (%)	Energy consumption (GWh)	Execution time (sec)
Configuration 1: 11,000 resources per Cell	1	2,419,200	2,407,079	33.86% (78.38%)	34.19% (89.86%)	90.52	1.25502	1870.03
	2	4,838,400	4,838,400	33.23% (79.61%)	30.68% (79.19%)	50.51	2.60836	1704.74
	3	7,257,600	7,257,600	23.64% (72.77%)	26.3% (78.33%)	37.4	3.26585	1776.24
	4	9,676,800	9,676,800	35.19% (77.15%)	34.24% (86.47%)	31.54	5.48662	1866.63
	8	19,353,600	19,314,339	50.62% (79.25%)	32.36% (84.5%)	58.11	10.68841	2772.45
Configuration 2: 110,000 resources per Cell	1	2,419,200	2,419,200	1.35% (59.01%)	3.52% (83.91%)	19.65	2.82534	4110.54
	2	4,838,400	4,838,400	1.48% (63.73%)	3.08% (72.52%)	14.22	5.78658	4198.38
	3	7,257,600	7,257,600	1.12% (57.6%)	2.63% (73.35%)	16.22	8.11747	4322.67
	4	9,676,800	9,676,800	1.39% (57.92%)	3.49% (79.06%)	17.44	11.93687	4906.20
	8	19,353,600	19,353,600	1.3% (56.16%)	3.34% (78.81%)	17.63	23.13896	5043.66

(continued)

Table 5.5 (continued)

Configuration	Cells	Submitted tasks	Accepted tasks	Average processor utilisation (over active servers)	Average accelerator utilisation (over active servers)	Average network utilisation (%)	Energy consumption (GWh)	Execution time (sec)
Configuration 3: 1,100,000 resources per Cell	1	2,419,200	2,419,200	0.13% (52.58%)	0.35% (75.92%)	19.82	20.14322	42,716.98
	2	4,838,400	4,838,400	0.14% (58.84%)	0.3% (68.39%)	14.18	40.37729	49,864.84
	3	7,257,600	7,257,600	0.11% (47.56%)	0.26% (61.58%)	16.22	60.06821	46,116.78
	4	9,676,800	9,676,800	0.14% (50.34%)	0.35% (69.99%)	17.68	81.01169	45,414.01
	8	19,353,600	19,353,600	0.13% (48.79%)	0.34% (70.09%)	17.89	161.36398	47,184.41

underlying resources. Since accelerators are more efficient in terms of computational efficiency and energy consumption, the system's choice is apparent.

It can also be seen that the total number of rejected tasks was very low (~0.05%), but the total estimated energy consumption of the cloud was close to the estimations of the traditional delivery system, due to the utilisation of the energy-efficient accelerators. Thus, the SOSM- based cloud environment was able to execute more tasks consuming almost equal energy. This was expected, since the SOSM selects the most efficient resources, executing the task faster, thus freeing those resources faster, and consequently leading to more tasks being accepted.

In order to examine the energy efficiency of the two resource allocation techniques in more detail, the ratio of the total energy consumption of the data centre over the number of accepted tasks was computed for all experiments. In Table 5.6, the number of Wh that is consumed per task for all configurations is presented. It can be observed that the number of Wh per task is substantially smaller when the SOSM engine is used. This is due to the fact that when the SOSM engine is not used, the resources that are utilised are selected randomly, while with the SOSM engine the resources

Table 5.6 Ratio of the total energy consumption of the cloud over the number of accepted tasks for all configurations

Configuration	Cells	Wh per task without SOSM	Wh per task with SOSM
Configuration 1: 11,000 resources per Cell	1	3030.26314	521.38713
	2	1633.66523	539.09557
	3	1268.57330	449.99035
	4	1044.89027	566.98702
	8	1333.53448	553.39248
Configuration 2: 110,000 resources per Cell	1	15,744.33657	1167.88194
	2	10,735.85269	1195.96974
	3	6239.39226	1118.47856
	4	4842.13695	1233.55551
	8	6982.59563	1195.58945
Configuration 3: 1,100,000 resources per Cell	1	142,955.84119	8326.39716
	2	93,556.77024	8345.17402
	3	53,754.62934	8276.59419
	4	39,736.79489	8371.74376
	8	60,682.07036	8337.67258

are selected by the system, according to the predefined strategies; thus, the most energy efficient solution is always chosen.

In Figs. 5.6 and 5.7, time-dependent charts are presented for the last experiment of the third configuration (eight Cells, 1,100,000 servers per Cell). In Fig. 5.6, the energy consumption, the processor utilisation, the accelerator utilisation, and the network utilisation of the cloud are presented with respect to the simulated time for the traditional centralised cloud service delivery. In Fig. 5.7, the energy consumption, the processor utilisation, the accelerator utilisation, and the network utilisation of the cloud are presented through the simulation time when using the SOSM engine.

5.5   CONCLUSION

This chapter presented the work towards demonstrating the scalability of the CloudLightning simulation framework. Cloud simulation tools are examined, since demonstrating scalability in hyperscale clouds is unfeasible. The design and implementation of the CloudLightning simulation framework were presented, a framework that overcomes the limitations of the existing simulation platforms. The main innovations of the framework lie in the fact that it is implemented for parallel computing systems (using MPI and OpenMP), it is based on a time-advancing loop instead of a discrete sequence of events, it allows the integration of dynamic resource allocation systems such as SOSM, and it supports hybrid CPU-accelerator resources. Finally, the CloudLightning Simulator was developed to be easily extensible, since the time-advancing execution model allows the integration of any strategies or phenomena observed in cloud environments.

From the experiments that were performed, the CloudLightning simulator was found to be capable of simulating clouds with large number of resources. Different executions were performed with the traditional cloud delivery system and with the use of the SOSM framework, for a various number of resources and Cells. Both the simulation platform and the SOSM framework were found to be scalable; simulations up to 8,800,000 hardware resources grouped into eight Cells were performed, only limited by the available hardware used for experimentation. SOSM was found to provide a more balanced distribution of tasks on the available hardware resources, with a much lower number of total rejected tasks. The energy consumption was found to be equivalent to the energy consumed when simulating a traditional cloud delivery system; however, the SOSM system

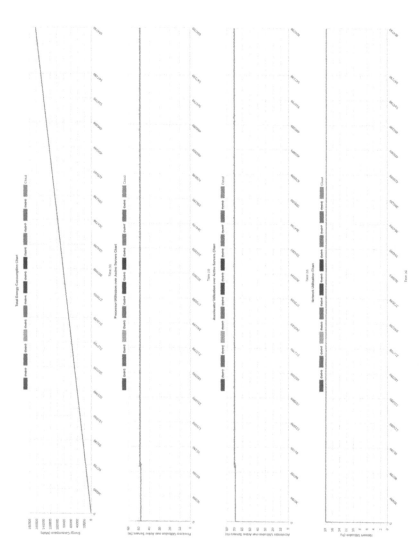

Fig. 5.7 Energy consumption, processor, accelerator, and network utilisation of the cloud over time for the SOSM simulation

was able to service a significantly larger number of tasks. Thus, the energy consumed per task in the SOSM system was substantially reduced compared to the traditional approach.

The CloudLightning Simulator and Simulator Visualization Tool are available for download under the Apache 2 open source licence at https://bitbucket.org/cloudlightning/cloudlightning-simulator and https://bitbucket.org/cloudlightning/cl-simulatorvisualization, respectively.

5.6   CHAPTER 5 RELATED CLOUDLIGHTNING READINGS

1. Byrne, J., Svorobej, S., Giannoutakis, K., Tzovaras, D., Byrne, P. J., Östberg, P. O., et al. (2017). A review of cloud computing simulation platforms and related environments. In *Proceedings of the 7th International Conference on Cloud Computing and Services Science (CLOSER 2017)* (pp. 679–691). SCITEPRESS-Science and Technology Publications, Lda.

2. Filelis-Papadopoulos, C. K., Gravvanis, G. A., & Kyziropoulos, P. E. (2017). A framework for simulating large scale cloud infrastructures. *Future Generation Computer Systems.* https://doi.org/10.1016/j.future.2017.06.017

3. Filelis-Papadopoulos, C. K., Gravvanis, G. A., & Morrison, J. P. (2017). CloudLightning simulation and evaluation roadmap. In *Proceedings of the 1st International Workshop on Next Generation of Cloud Architectures*, Vol. 2. ACM.

4. Filelis-Papadopoulos, C. K., Grylonakis, E. N. G., Kyziropoulos, P. E., Gravvanis, G. A., & Morrison, J. P. (2016). Characterization of hardware in self-managing self-organizing Cloud environment. In *Proceedings of the 20th Pan-Hellenic Conference on Informatics*, Vol. 56. ACM.

5. Filelis-Papadopoulos, C. K., Giannoutakis, K. M., & Gravvanis, G. A. (2017). Large-scale simulation of a self-organizing self-management cloud computing framework. *The Journal of Supercomputing.* https://doi.org/10.1007/s11227-017-2143-2

6. Giannoutakis, K. M., Makaratzis, A. T., Tzovaras, D., Filelis-Papadopoulos, C. K., & Gravvanis, G. A. (2017, April). On the power consumption modeling for the simulation of Heterogeneous HPC Clouds. In *Proceedings of the 1st International Workshop on Next Generation of Cloud Architectures*, Vol. 1. ACM.

7. Lynn, T., Gourinovitch, A., Byrne, J., Byrne, P. J., Svorobej, S., Giannoutakis, K., et al. (2017). A preliminary systematic review of computer science literature on cloud computing research using Open Source simulation platforms. In *Proceedings of the 7th International Conference on Cloud Computing and Services Science (CLOSER 2017)* (pp. 537–545). SCITEPRESS-Science and Technology Publications, Lda.
8. Makaratzis, A. T., Giannoutakis, K. M., & Tzovaras, D. (2017). Energy modeling in cloud simulation frameworks. *Future Generation Computer Systems.* https://doi.org/10.1016/j.future.2017.06.016

NOTES

1. https://www.spec.org/power_ssj2008/results/res2016q2/power_ssj2008-20160607-00734.html
2. http://spec.org/power_ssj2008/results/res2016q2/power_ssj2008-20160328-00719.html

REFERENCES

Barroso, L. A., Clidaras, J., & Hoelzle, U. (2013). *The datacenter as a computer: An introduction to the design of warehouse-scale machines.* Morgan & Claypool. https://doi.org/10.2200/S00516ED2V01Y201306CAC024

Beloglazov, A., & Buyya, R. (2012). Optimal online deterministic algorithms and adaptive heuristics for energy and performance efficient dynamic consolidation of virtual machines in cloud data centers. *Concurrency and Computation: Practice & Experience, 24*(13), 1397–1420. https://doi.org/10.1002/cpe.1867

Byrne, J., Svorobej, S., Giannoutakis, K. M., Tzovaras, D., Byrne, P., Ostberg, P. O., et al. (2017). A review of cloud computing simulation platforms and related environments. In *The 7th International Conference on Cloud Computing and Services Science* (pp. 651–663).

Calheiros, R. N., Ranjan, R., Beloglazov, A., De Rose, C. A. F., & Buyya, R. (2011). CloudSim: A toolkit for modeling and simulation of cloud computing environments and evaluation of resource provisioning algorithms. *Software: Practice and Experience, 41*(1), 23–50. https://doi.org/10.1002/spe.995

Cisco Global Cloud Index: Forecast and Methodology, 2015–2020. (2016). Retrieved from https://www.cisco.com/c/dam/en/us/solutions/collateral/service-provider/global-cloud-index-gci/white-paper-c11-738085.pdf

Dagum, L., & Menon, R. (1998). OpenMP: An industry standard API for shared memory programming. *IEEE Computational Science and Engineering, 5*(1), 46–55. https://doi.org/10.1109/99.660313

Filelis-Papadopoulos, C., Xiong, H., Spataru, A., Castañe, G., Dapeng, D., Gravvanis, G., et al. (2017). A generic framework supporting self-organisation and self-management in hierarchical systems. In *Proceedings of the International Symposium on Parallel and Distributed Computing.*

Filelis-Papadopoulos, C. K., Giannoutakis, K. M., Gravvanis, G. A., & Tzovaras, D. (2017). Large-scale simulation of a self-organizing self-management cloud computing framework. *The Journal of Supercomputing.* https://doi.org/10.1007/s11227-017-2143-2

Filelis-Papadopoulos, C. K., Gravvanis, G. A., & Kyziropoulos, P. E. (2017). A framework for simulating large scale cloud infrastructures. *Future Generation Computer Systems.* https://doi.org/10.1016/j.future.2017.06.017

Filelis-Papadopoulos, C. K., Gravvanis, G. A., & Morrison, J. P. (2017). CloudLightning simulation and evaluation roadmap. In *Proceedings of the 1st International Workshop on Next Generation of Cloud Architectures* (pp. 2:1–2:6). New York, NY: ACM. https://doi.org/10.1145/3068126.3068128

Giannoutakis, K. M., Makaratzis, A. T., Tzovaras, D., Filelis-Papadopoulos, C. K., & Gravvanis, G. A. (2017). On the power consumption modeling for the simulation of heterogeneous HPC clouds. In *Proceedings of the 1st International Workshop on Next Generation of Cloud Architectures* (pp. 1:1–1:6). New York, NY: ACM. https://doi.org/10.1145/3068126.3068127

Gropp, W., Lusk, E., Doss, N., & Skjellum, A. (1996). A high-performance, portable implementation of the MPI message passing interface standard. *Parallel Computing, 22*(6), 789–828. https://doi.org/10.1016/0167-8191(96)00024-5

Gupta, S. K. S., Gilbert, R. R., Banerjee, A., Abbasi, Z., Mukherjee, T., & Varsamopoulos, G. (2011). GDCSim: A tool for analyzing green data center design and resource management techniques. In *2011 International Green Computing Conference and Workshops* (pp. 1–8). https://doi.org/10.1109/IGCC.2011.6008612

Kliazovich, D., Bouvry, P., & Khan, S. U. (2012). GreenCloud: A packet-level simulator of energy-aware cloud computing data centers. *The Journal of Supercomputing, 62*(3), 1263–1283. https://doi.org/10.1007/s11227-010-0504-1

Makaratzis, A., Khan, M., Giannoutakis, K., Elster, A., & Tzovaras, D. (2017). GPU power modeling of HPC applications for the simulation of heterogeneous clouds. In *International Conference on Parallel Processing and Applied Mathematics.*

Mars, J. (2012). *Rethinking the architecture of warehouse-scale computers* (Doctoral dissertation, University of Virginia). https://doi.org/10.18130/V30N5R

Nunez, A., Vazquez-Poletti, J. L., Caminero, A. C., Castañe, G. G., Carretero, J., & Llorente, I. M. (2012). iCanCloud: A flexible and scalable cloud infrastructure simulator. *Journal of Grid Computing, 10*(1), 185–209. https://doi.org/10.1007/s10723-012-9208-5

SPEC. (2008). Standard performance evaluation corporation, server power and performance characteristics. Retrieved from http://www.spec.org/powerssj2008/

Tian, W., Zhao, Y., Xu, M., Zhong, Y., & Sun, X. (2015). A toolkit for modeling and simulation of real-time virtual machine allocation in a cloud data center. *IEEE Transactions on Automation Science and Engineering, 12*(1), 153–161. https://doi.org/10.1109/TASE.2013.2266338

Tighe, M., Keller, G., Bauer, M., & Lutfiyya, H. (2012). DCSim: A data centre simulation tool for evaluating dynamic virtualized resource management. In *2012 8th International Conference on Network and Service Management (CNSM) and 2012 Workshop on Systems Virtualization Management (SVM)* (pp. 385–392).

CHAPTER 6

Concluding Remarks

Theo Lynn and John P. Morrison

Abstract Traditionally, access to high performance computing was restricted by architectural complexity, availability of trained personnel, and budgetary issues. At the same time, research suggests that existing measures for greater data centre energy efficiencies will reach theoretical and practical limits in the near future. This concluding chapter briefly discusses the potential of (i) cloud computing to disrupt the high performance computing sector, and (ii) new heterogeneous cloud architectures, based on the concepts of self-organisation, self-management, and the separation of concerns, to disrupt extant cloud resource management approaches.

Keywords Disruptive innovation • Cloud computing • High performance computing • HPC in the cloud

T. Lynn (✉)
Irish Centre for Cloud Computing (IC4), Dublin City University,
Dublin, Ireland
e-mail: theo.lynn@dcu.ie

J. P. Morrison
Department of Computer Science, University College Cork, Cork, Ireland
e-mail: j.morrison@cs.ucc.ie

© The Author(s) 2018   151
T. Lynn et al. (eds.), *Heterogeneity, High Performance Computing,
Self-Organization and the Cloud*, Palgrave Studies in Digital
Business & Enabling Technologies,
https://doi.org/10.1007/978-3-319-76038-4_6

Clayton Christensen, in his seminal study on the disk drive industry, identified two types of technological change. Sustaining technologies sustained the industry's rate of improvement in product performance and ranged in difficulty from incremental to radical, whereas so-called disruptive innovations redefined performance trajectories and consistently resulted in the failure of the industry's leading firms (Christensen 1997). Cloud computing continues to transform, and democratise access to, the use of information and communications technology infrastructure. Organisations of all sizes and sectors, as well as the general public, are able to exploit the advantages of the agility and scalability (up and down) inherent in cloud computing to work more efficiently, reduce Information Technology (IT) costs (including IT capital expenditure, maintenance and support costs, and related environmental costs), support resilience and business continuity, and growth (Hogan et al. 2011; Low et al. 2011; Buyya et al. 2009; Leimbach et al. 2014). This book is about disruptive potential—the (i) the potential of cloud computing to disrupt the high performance computing (HPC) sector and (ii) the potential of a new heterogeneous cloud architecture based on the concepts of self-organisation, self-management, and the separation of concerns to disrupt extant cloud resource management approaches.

For a significant portion of the last half-century, HPC exploited relatively established trajectories of performance; single-thread processor clock frequency was viewed as the main driving factor behind increasing computational performance. Manufacturers of such processors, and Intel in particular, delivered consistent improvements in performance until hitting a scientific "power wall" for single-core processors at the turn of the century. With the levelling off of single-thread processor performance, the industry sought to sustain performance trajectories by combining multiple Central Processing Unit (CPU) cores on one chip to achieve performance gains. While multi-core architectures achieve performance gains, efficient parallel computation on multiple cores provided discrete challenges for the HPC end user community. More recently, the use of different types of processor has been exploited to address this issue. As different compute resources can have different properties, applications with diverse characteristics can be executed quicker and more efficiently using these processors.

Heterogeneous architectures support these specialist processors as co-processors to a host processor; the host processor can complete one instruction stream, while the co-processor can complete a different instruction stream or different type of stream (Eijkhout et al. 2016). While such heterogeneous resources can provide new measures of performance, for example, energy efficiency, both technically and culturally the HPC community remains focused on maximising the (effective) processing speed of a given architecture to orders of magnitude greater than general-purpose computing. Whereas each evolution of the processor architecture was relatively novel in the context of difficult HPC applications, it was not disruptive. To paraphrase Christensen (1997), the customers of the leading HPC supplier led them towards these achievements. These sustaining technologies did not precipitate failure by incumbents or significant changes in the HPC industry structure. Size still matters. The HPC community remains dominated by a relatively small number of suppliers catering for a relatively small number of large organisations requiring significant investments in infrastructure. For the most part, access to HPC remains restricted by architectural complexity, availability of trained personnel, and budgetary issues (Intersect360 Research 2014).

In the last few years, cloud service providers (CSPs) have sought to enter the HPC market; however, HPC has remained one of the smallest segments in the market. This can be explained by both technical and cultural perceptions on the nature of HPC and the efficacy of cloud computing architectures to deliver high performance. From a technical perspective, many HPC workloads are not ready to run on today's cloud architectures, and provisioning of HPC clusters in the cloud still typically requires deep IT knowledge. Similarly, many in the HPC community do not believe a general-purpose distributed architecture designed for multi-tenancy, horizontal scaling, and minimal interference with physical infrastructure can deliver the performance expectations for HPC. And this may be correct.

However, there are classes of HPC users who do not need maximum performance, and this goes to the core of the disruptive potential of cloud computing for HPC. Cloud computing creates new markets and value networks for organisations (and individuals) who cannot afford or cannot gain convenient access to traditional HPC infrastructure such as supercomputers, who have loosely coupled workloads that can be scaled horizontally, and/or have pent-up HPC demand and find it difficult to burst capacity for overflow or surge workloads with their existing HPC infrastructure. Given the impact HPC has on scientific discovery and innovation, dramatically increasing access and use of HPC through the cloud to this wider community of low-end consumers or non-consumers has the potential to drive significant societal and economic impact.

At the same time, it is questionable whether the economic model of conventional hyperscale cloud computing is sustainable in the long term. Not from a business or technology perspective but from an environmental perspective. The IT sector accounts for a significant portion of global electricity with some estimates at approximately 7% (Corcoran and Andrae 2013). Data centres have an extremely energy-intensive profile. For example, a study conducted for the US Department of Energy estimates that data centres consume 10–50 times the energy per floor space of a typical commercial office building and collectively (Darrow and Hedman 2009). In 2014, data centres accounted for 1.8% of total US electricity consumption driven by increased Internet usage and the rise of cloud computing (Shehabi et al. 2016). Research suggests that the data centre sector, and hyperscale data operators specifically, has taken significant measures to improve energy efficiency including increasing server productivity and utilisation and efficiency improvements in storage, network, and data centre infrastructure operations such as cooling (Shehabi et al. 2016). Despite these initiatives, the environmental impact of Information and Communications Technologies (ICT) operations, data centres, and cloud energy usage remains a significant concern and increased focus of policy makers and civic society.

Research suggests that existing measures for greater data centre energy efficiencies will reach theoretical and practical limits in the near future, and therefore cloud computing especially needs to look beyond its current model of using one-size-fits-all hardware towards optimising hardware for specific workloads (Shehabi et al. 2016). Such optimisation is central to the heterogeneous cloud; however, such a vision for cloud computing increases the complexity of managing cloud infrastructure dramatically. As such, a new paradigm for cloud computing architectural design is required.

This book presents one possible architectural design, CloudLightning, for managing heterogeneous clouds based on self-organisation, self-management, and the separation of concerns. CloudLightning is a fundamentally different architecture to the homogeneous cloud platforms prevalent today. Specifically, it both accommodates workload variation through optimised heterogeneous hardware and hides this complexity from enterprise application developers and end users, thus providing a different package of attributes including not only hardware performance but energy efficiency, ease of management, and ease of use as well. CloudLightning's disruptive potential is the new performance trajectory that such attributes create.

REFERENCES

Buyya, R., Yeo, C. S., Venugopal, S., Broberg, J., & Brandic, I. (2009). Cloud computing and emerging IT platforms: Vision, hype, and reality for delivering computing as the 5th utility. *Future Generation Computer Systems, 25*(6), 599–616.

Christensen, C. M. (1997). *The innovator's dilemma: When new technologies cause great firms to fail.* Cambridge, MA: Harvard Business School Press.

Corcoran, P., & Andrae, A. (2013). *Emerging trends in electricity consumption for consumer ICT.* Tech. Rep., National University of Ireland, Galway, Connacht, Ireland. Retrieved October 24, 2016, from https://aran.library.nuigalway.ie/xmlui/handle/10379/3563

Darrow, K., & Hedman, B. (2009). *Opportunities for combined heat and power in data centres.* Arlington, VA: ICF International.

Eijkhout, V., van de Geijn, R., & Chow, E. (2016). Introduction to high performance scientific computing. *Zenodo.* https://doi.org/10.5281/zenodo.49897

Hogan, M., Liu, F., Sokol, A., & Tong, J. (2011). *NIST cloud computing standards roadmap.* NIST Special Publication, 35.

Intersect360 Research. (2014). *Worldwide high performance computing 2013: Total Market Model and 2014–18 forecast.* Sunnyvale, CA.

Leimbach, T., Hallinan, D., Bachlechner, D., Weber, A., Jaglo, M., Hennen, L., et al. (2014). Potential and impacts of cloud computing services and social network websites (STOA Cloud Computing—Study). Retrieved October 26, 2017, from http://www.europarl.europa.eu/RegData/etudes/etudes/join/2014/513546/IPOL-JOIN_ET(2014)513546_EN.pdf

Low, C., Chen, Y., & Wu, M. (2011). Understanding the determinants of cloud computing adoption. *Industrial Management & Data Systems, 111*(7), 1006–1023.

Shehabi, A., Smith, S. J., Horner, N., Azevedo, I., Brown, R., Koomey, J., et al. (2016). *United States data centre energy usage report LBNL-1005775.* Berkeley, CA: Lawrence Berkeley National Laboratory.

INDEX[1]

---

[1] Note: Page numbers followed by 'n' refer to notes.

© The Author(s) 2018   157
T. Lynn et al. (eds.), *Heterogeneity, High Performance Computing,
Self-Organization and the Cloud*, Palgrave Studies in Digital
Business & Enabling Technologies,
https://doi.org/10.1007/978-3-319-76038-4